# ALCOI
# RECOVERY

The Short Term in Order to Make You a Simple
and Effective Alcohol Addiction

(How to Recover From Alcohol Addiction and
Alcohol Abuse for Life)

**Cedric Rodriguez**

Published by Tomas Edwards

*Alcohol Recovery: The Short Term in Order to Make You a Simple and Effective Alcohol Addiction (How to Recover From Alcohol Addiction and Alcohol Abuse for Life)*

ISBN 978-1-990373-32-9

Legal & Disclaimer

The information contained in this book is not designed to replace or take the place of any form of medicine or professional medical advice. The information in this book has been provided for educational and entertainment purposes only.

The information contained in this book has been compiled from sources deemed reliable, and it is accurate to the best of the Author's knowledge; however, the Author cannot guarantee its accuracy and validity and cannot be held liable for any errors or omissions. Changes are periodically made to this book. You must consult your doctor or get professional medical advice before using any of the suggested remedies, techniques, or information in this book.

Upon using the information contained in this book, you agree to hold harmless the Author from and against any damages, costs, and expenses, including any legal fees potentially resulting from the application of any of the information provided by this guide. This disclaimer applies to any damages or injury caused by the use and application, whether directly or indirectly, of any advice or information presented, whether for breach of contract, tort, negligence, personal injury, criminal intent, or under any other cause of action.

You agree to accept all risks of using the information presented inside this book. You need to consult a professional medical practitioner in order to ensure you are both able and healthy enough to participate in this program.

# Table of Contents

# Introduction

Alcohol is a very ancient drink that has been consumed for thousands of years by almost all civilizations. Alcoholic beverages are an important part of many social events. A lot of us resort to a glass of wine at home after a hard day. So how do you know when an innocent drink turns into a dangerous addiction? Can alcohol actually be good for you? What is a safe dose of alcohol? We set out on a quest to find out the answers to all these questions and more.

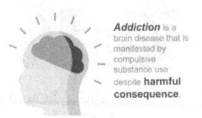

**Addiction** is a brain disease that is manifested by compulsive substance use despite **harmful consequence**.

So can alcohol actually be used as a medicine? The answer is only in rare cases. If we are dealing with a heart attack, liver or kidney colic and there are no medications available, then we can use alcohol. One tablespoon of vodka or cognac will help eliminate the vessel and muscular spasms thus improving the patient's condition until the ambulance arrives. However the relaxation effect caused by alcohol is very short and is followed by the phase of prolonged vessel and muscular spasms.

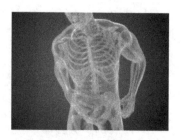

What effects do alcoholic beverages have on blood pressure? They raise it. This is exactly the reason why alcohol actually helps those who have hypotonia, one or two tablespoons of cognac can resuscitate a person with low blood pressure. However, the World Health Organization does not recommend for doctors to advise their patients to take any alcoholic beverages as their medicine. Longstanding research shows that the cause of 20% of all cases of hypertension is alcohol, especially beer and vodka. Thus, if a man consumes more than 5 oz of wine or 2 oz of vodka a day, the risk of developing hypertension increases to 40%; in the same case for women the risk increases to 90%! So it is much safer to increase blood pressure not with alcohol but with coffee, tea, dark chocolate, or ginseng tincture.

It's a known fact that natural dry wines are beneficial for us. What is this effect due to? The skin and seeds of red type of grape contain a substance that has a huge antioxidant effect. When we eat that type of grapes or drink wine made out of it, this substance prevents the development of cardio-vascular and oncological diseases, it slows down the age changes in the brain and in the motor function thus extending the life span and delaying the body's aging. Besides that, alcoholic beverages improve digestion and prevent building up of cholesterol on the vascular walls. But all of this is true only when alcohol is consumed in moderate amounts. Consumption of alcohol in large amounts leads to heart pathologies and hypertension. So it's much safer to lower cholesterol with the help of physical activities and rational diet, which are just as effective as alcohol.

How is it that the French eat a lot of fatty foods, drink beer and at the same time live long lives and suffer from cardio-vascular diseases 40% less than the Americans? The secret of the "French paradox" is not only in consuming wine regularly, but also in their lifestyle and peculiarities of their diet. Besides wine and cheese the French consume a large amount of vegetables, fruit, verdure, olive oil and seafood. This diet supplies the body with lipoproteins of high density, unsaturated fats, vitamins and microelements, which cause a powerful antioxidant effect, protecting the body's cells from damages by free radicals. Furthermore, the residents of South France actively consume seaweed, which contains substances that improve the biological properties of blood (decrease the formation of clots and stimulate disintegration of fats).

What amount of alcohol is considered a safe dose? In France, Italy, and Hungary this number would traditionally be higher than that in Sweden or Norway, for example. But talking about the common dose, the World Health Organization recommends for men to consume not more than 30 ml of pure alcohol, which is about 1.5 bottles of beer or 2 shots of vodka a day, and for women - 20 ml of pure alcohol per day, which is 1 bottle of beer or 1 shot of vodka. The doctors also recommend refraining from drinking alcoholic beverages at least two days a week.

So why is the safe dose for women lower than the one for men? This is explained by the fact that women have less water in their body than men do. Besides, the element responsible for the disintegration of alcohol located in the stomach is less active in women. Therefore the processing of alcoholic beverages is slower in female bodies making the ladies more receptive to alcohol.

Why is it that some people get a headache after a glass of red wine, but feel fine after drinking white wine? This reaction could be caused by individual intolerance of sulfur dioxide - the substance that is added to red dry wines for longer storage. This preservative can cause immediate redness of the face and strong migraines. This does not happen when consuming white wines because there is no sulfur dioxide added to them according to their preparation technology.

How safe are the low-alcohol sparkling drinks so popular among the younger people? Easy math allows us to see that this category of drinks is not so harmless. Most of them contain 8% alcohol. If you multiply this number by 0.33, which is the contents of one bottle, then we get about 27 ml of pure alcohol. For women it is already over their daily limit, and usually few stop at just one bottle a day. Besides these drinks usually contain carbon dioxide, which contributes to faster absorption of alcohol into blood due to which intoxication happens almost after the first sip.

What are the consequences of immoderate consumption of beer? Beer, just as any other alcoholic beverage, first of all affects the liver, causing toxic hepatitis and alcohol cirrhosis. Namely these two diseases have the leading positions in beer countries such as Germany, where beer is consumed often and in big amounts, up to 3 liters per night.

Former smokers complain that after having a drink they get the desire to smoke again. Why does it happen? Usually this happens to those who managed to say no to the harmful habit but haven't coped with the psychological smoking addiction. Once the former smoker goes to the party where a lot of people smoke, he or she can experience what a former drug addict would feel if he appeared in a surrounding where they used to do drugs. Just one glance at the familiar surroundings is enough to be overtaken with the associative habit. Under the influence of alcohol, the memory draws the pictures of the past that are so vivid that the former smoker can actually feel the taste and smell of tobacco. Besides being in the state of euphoria (after having a couple of drinks) a person already can not critically assess his or her actions and breaks their own promises without thinking twice. Typically we smoke more cigarettes than usual in this condition. As a result the toxic effect of alcohol is intensified by several times, hence a more severe hangover.

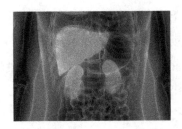

What medicines could be combined with alcohol? Alcohol is not compatible with any medications, especially cardio-stimulants, tranquilizers, antidepressants, and beta-blockers. Losing conciseness is the least of the potential consequences. Sometimes alcohol can intensify the effects of the medications by so much that it can lead to coma or even sudden death. Alcoholic beverages are also not compatible with diuretic medications. Combined with wine or beer diuretics remove such a big amount of microelements out of your body that it can lead to heart malfunctions. Even the commonplace aspirin should not be chased with alcoholic drinks - such experiments can lead to stomach ulcer. A vast amount of complications can be caused by combining alcohol with antibiotics. Not all medications enter our body in active form. A lot of them start acting only after they pass the stage of disintegration in the liver. Alcohol requires disintegration too, and thus once both medications and alcohol enter our body at the same time, both of these substances start to compete. As a result the active ingredient of the medication gets to our body under-oxidized, which most often leads to allergic reactions.

Why is it that some people become placid and talkative after having a drink, and others become withdrawn and aggressive?

10

In spite of the person's character, age and mood, the alcohol slows down the function of the nervous system. Two minutes after having a drink, the alcohol reaches the frontal lobe of the brain leading to the disruption of the most of neuro-chemical bonds. You become absent-minded, the thoughts become chaotic, and the mood becomes elevated and cheerful. Although this state of euphoria is short-term, soon the phase of inhibition comes, during which the intoxicated person looses restraint and common sense and their conversations and actions become inappropriate. Usually alcohol affects healthy people as an emotional equalizer: a closed-off person brightens up after a glass of wine, a talkative one quiets down, an aggressive one calms down. Although sometimes unexpected reactions happen, which are usually predetermined by peculiarities of the person's nervous system. One fact remains though, if after having a drink you become aggressive, you should stay away from drinking.

A lot of people consider alcohol the best cure of stress, is that true? Alcohol is the most simple and accessible tranquilizer. However it does not relieve stress, otherwise everyone would be drinking their problems away. Fortunately, this does not happen since for most people alcohol is just a mediator, something of a relaxing element, which allows them to talk frankly, to pour their heart out to the closest friend, neighbor, and fellow traveler. However the doctors consider jogging just as effective due to the increased production of energy in our body when under stress. That is why when we start stressing out we cannot stay in one place: we pace the room, pull at our hair, talk emotionally. Therefore it would be quite logical to get rid of the excess energy at the gym rather than at the bar.

Are there any rules one should follow when drinking? The first rule is never drink on an empty stomach. If you don't eat anything prior, alcohol is absorbed freely by the stomach and quickly gets into blood causing immediate and very strong intoxication. This is why dietitians recommend eating something greasy beforehand. The second rule is to start the party up with aperitif, a small drink before you eat to stimulate the appetite. If you have a little bit of wine, vodka or martini first, not only will you stimulate the appetite, but you will also make the fermentative system work more actively. The third rule is if you have to change a drink make sure to drink higher proof drinks each time. Processing high-proof drinks requires a lot of the ferment responsible for breaking up alcohol hence if you chase cognac with champagne you will cause the deficit of this ferment. Because of that, the low-proof drink gets into our body unbroken without obstruction causing strong intoxication.

What kind of food should you have with strong drinks? Dry wines should be followed by fruit, cheese, salads, non-greasy types of meat, and fish. Drinks with 80 proof and higher go best with greasier and heavier foods - pork, lamb, red caviar, potatoes, salads with high-calories sauces. This will help slow down the absorption of alcohol and improve the digestion of food since alcohol helps break up fats. It is desirable to have fresh lemons available during a long get-together. The acid contained by them is an excellent decomposer of alcohol therefore you can chase your drinks with cut up pieces of this sour fruit or have a glass of water mixed with lemon juice. You might want to get rid of sparkling sweet drinks since sugar and carbon dioxide contained by them increase the absorption speed of alcohol. This is the same reason why you should not chase sparkling wines with chocolate.

What is alcohol poisoning? What are its symptoms and what precautions should be taken to save the person who got alcohol poisoning? Alcohol poisoning happens after consumption of more than 500 ml of vodka. Most people's body natural reaction to such an amount of toxic substances is vomiting, but more than 30% of alcohol drinkers are missing this reflex, therefore if the body is exposed to a large amount of ethanol, it undergoes the strongest alcohol intoxication: alcohol paralyzes the nervous system which leads to comatose condition and if left unattended can lead to death in several hours. This is why if you find someone unconscious with a distinct alcohol smell, pale, perspirating, having hurried breathing, not reacting to any outside stimuli, having weak pulse and uneven heartbeat, call the ambulance immediately.

# Chapter 1: Illness Or Weakness?

If a person nevertheless admits himself sick, and we see that this can only be admitted by yourself, then such a person can abandon the feeling of shame for what happened. Alcoholism is a disease of altered morality. After a binge, a person is immensely ashamed of what happened. People are surprised; why wasn't it a shame while drinking? Under the influence of craving, it was also embarrassing, but "craving" (the medical term - compulsive drive) is regarded by a sick mind as one of the natural needs. The ancient mechanism comes into force: "ashamed, but what to do?" After getting intoxicated, the shame goes away completely. Man is already becoming another creature. But after a binge, the feeling of shame is double.

When ashamed of a problem, patients lose the opportunity not only to solve it but even to ever begin to solve it. It is impossible to cope with what you are ashamed of. An alcoholic is like a person sweeping cockroaches under a sofa, just to not see them. He will be forced to cover this topic of conversation all his life either with silly laughter (often you have to see adults begin to giggle like schoolchildren when this topic is mentioned), or theorizing (resonant reasoning about the philosophy, biochemistry and historical roots of the process), or simply gross denial. One way or another, but after two or three phrases, you'll have to hear something like: "Well, okay, enough about that!"

People involved in the fate of the patient, also do not really like to talk about this topic. They believe that once again, it is not worth provoking. The man already looks repentant. Yes, and they themselves

18

do not like it, it is better to forget and live on.

However, forgetting will not work, not only because it is impossible to forget, but also because soon it will happen again. And again, we will treat the consequences without affecting what causes them.

If an alcoholic pleads ill, then the feeling of shame becomes surmountable. No need to be ashamed of disease. After all, no one is ashamed of bronchial asthma or hypertension. Yes, you can't talk to everyone about this topic. Many will react incorrectly, but it is not necessary for everyone.

- There are relatives, close people who already know everything, and if they don't know something, "tell about yourself" is a normal phrase with close relations.

- There are people who have dealt with this problem. They will react correctly;

they will neither laugh nor be rude. A conversation with such a person is extremely useful. Many of them want to share their experiences and will be grateful to those who want to listen to them.

- Finally, there are doctors, to understand the patient and show compassion for him is their professional duty. It is foolish to be ashamed of a doctor. In any case, if you do not step over the feeling of shame, you will not succeed at all. You do not get off the ground what you stand with your back to.

By admitting that he is ill, a person can give up the guilt. True, to refuse does not mean to lose. These feelings will not go away immediately and not forever. The important thing is that the patient ceases to take them into account in his logic. He understands that these are painful feelings. This is how his illness hides from him. Yes, alcoholism is a psychiatric illness, madness. But the madman is not guilty.

An alcoholic really feels eternally guilty. Sometimes, he even thinks that it's good that it will help him stop drinking. Others, as a rule, cultivate this feeling with good intentions, believing that this will bring the patient closer to sobriety, to treatment. It is customary to report the patient, scold, point out to him his shortcomings, in a word, to educate him as a small child. The effect is actually quite the opposite!

Firstly while a person considers himself guilty and not sick (and these are conflicting concepts), he will involuntarily seek excuses. An alcoholic turns into an unfortunate person who protects the one who kills him – alcohol. He is forced to constantly explain to himself and everyone why he drank? Alcoholic alibis begin to be built, one more ridiculous than the other (such a life, such a job, such a wife, etc.). People around start to argue on this subject: "it's not so bad, you couldn't even drink as I do." These disputes are endless and useless. There are no excuses because there are no accusations: Either you consider yourself sick - yes, this is insanity, but it is a disease, then the disease is to blame. No one is justified in the fact that he has a toothache, or there was an attack of radiculitis. Or you can retain your belief that it's not a disease, then it means that you live like that. Yes, we don't like it, but what you can do is your choice...

No one needs to theorize why a thief came and stole everything. Yes, because he is a thief! The question is, why it penetrated so easily? So there was no protection.

Secondly, as long as a person considers himself guilty, he will consider that they are offered not help, but punishment. If you are guilty, then they are punished! For the time being, an alcoholic refuses all manipulations and influences. He cannot afford help because he considers himself "not guilty enough." All talk on this topic is annoying. The perception of the topic is changing: advice is perceived as reproaches, jokes, as a mockery, the very word "alcoholic," invariably, as an insult.

"Why bother me?" is a very common question at this stage. One would like to answer: "why does a person go to the dentist?" It may even hurt there, but they don't drag him there by force, patients themselves turn. Such logic lasts until the guilt becomes so painful that it will be easier to get punishment. The punishment itself becomes desirable; it relieves for a time of guilt. After all, they're not punished twice. I drank again - and the topic was closed at a hospital once more.

The "poor fellow" did the procedure, and then the nightmare begins: we are so arranged that we cannot get what we did not expect. Once I went for punishment at the hospital - I received the punishment. This patient will be tormented all this time, suffer, torment himself and others, he should be bad - because he was punished! Sometimes, by the end of the year, the family begins to whisper: "He will definitely drink as soon as the treatment ends. Another drink! He pulled the emotional spring for a whole year, and now he let go ..." These events are part of alcohol mythology; everyone heard about a friend or relative who had everything turned out just like that. Such a result cannot be considered positive; it is only a change in the frequency of disruptions, and even then not always. This does not mean that you do not need to seek help. It is important to understand that the result is 90% dependent not on the method, but on what the patient himself was oriented to. If he is to blame, it means punishment; if he is sick, it is help, deliverance, after which he will become better.

Thirdly, as long as the alcoholic considers himself not sick, but guilty, he will be forced to make amends until he drinks. This is the curse of alcoholics - people who live on hard drinking. They not only drink heavily but also work, read, love impulsively, as if it was another binge for them. Jumping out of an alcoholic nightmare, experiencing an immense sense of guilt, such a person begins to involuntarily search for a feat. He needs exorbitant fatigue because only extreme fatigue will help get rid of guilt. How often you hear from patients: "Well, what an alcoholic I am, I work!"

Of course, you work, how you work! After all, you need to feed not only yourself but also your alcoholism. Unfortunately, thoughts will be. After all, we are talking about a disease, and it will develop. Increasing momentum, sooner or later, such a patient still reaches a certain limit of fatigue, and then another breakdown begins. This is a vicious circle, or rather a spiral leading down. In this arena, people move like circus horses for years and decades. Alcoholism is a very cunning host. He is not interested in the quick death of his slaves. Therefore, alcoholics live relatively long. If nothing bad happens - trauma, poisoning, and other causes of early mortality - an alcoholic can live up to 60 and 70 years. The truth is that all this time, he does not live, but feeds the disease. He studies, marries, has children, but all his life he is in two states - either unconsciously preparing for a binge, or is in it. There is only one way to jump from this carousel of madness - to admit that you are sick. In this case, sobriety is not a way to make amends, but a way to begin to live as intended. Each person was born for happiness, but an alcoholic cannot afford it.

While an alcoholic drinks, he dooms himself to an existence in which he is either unhappy or drunk. In sobriety, the alcoholic must be happy. Otherwise, he will get drunk - this is not a wish, but a medical recommendation, the possibility of saving a life!

By admitting that he is sick, a person can abandon feelings of shame and guilt. He can exchange them for dignity.

Sobriety is a virtue for those who understand. There is such a variation in this feeling. Do not be offended by a friend who, in response to a confession: "I haven't been drinking for six months," answers: "so what?" If you happen to talk to a person who has not been drinking for five years, he will answer something like: "I remember the first six months ... Well done, come on, keep t up!

This is real pride, not pompous, but special. Forgive those who do not understand this. Many of them are not alcoholics, they do not understand, and they do not need to understand this. And many of those who do not understand are sick people who still have not admitted this to themselves. We will pity them, God willing, and they will someday receive this pride.

The most important conclusion from recognizing yourself as a patient is a desire to stop drinking alcohol forever. That is, for life, any alcoholic beverage, in any quantity for any reason. In this case, we are talking about absolute sobriety.

In narcology, there are two cornerstones: the active participation of the patient and absolute sobriety as a result. If someone offers "dose control," "treatment without the knowledge," or any other "help" - this person cannot be called a doctor, no matter how he introduces himself.

The provision on absolute sobriety is not even a doctor's suggestion, but a requirement of a sick person! It is unlikely that anyone had heard that the patient persuaded the doctor to cure him not forever, but only temporarily. Nobody wants a recurrence of the disease. Usually, doctors are forced to avert their eyes and speak old words like the world: "medicine is not omnipotent ...", "we are doing everything possible ..." "I do not give guarantees, but I will try to help you ..." In these dialogues, patients are perplexed: "How so? I need an absolute result! Is it really impossible to achieve complete deliverance?"

A sick person is actively seeking help, requires it. He will go through all the experts, read a lot of literature, he will look for everything that can help him. Arguing like this: "Well, okay, I'm an alcoholic, leave me alone," "maybe I'm really sick, maybe I need to pause," the person contradicts himself.

Recognizing himself sick, the alcoholic transfers the situation from moral and ethical to medical. Therefore, the question: "And what if I am an alcoholic, I can't drink already?" By itself, this is meaningless. The doctor is not a lawyer and does not answer legal questions. Is it possible to cough? Can't you walk with a toothache? But what if sometimes, on holidays, I have a rash and a fever? What isn't it possible?

All in all, as opposed to other types of sickness, the cure starts and ends with you!

# Chapter 2: Determining The Triggers

## To Your Alcohol Problem

Millions of people around the world consume alcohol in one form or the other. Yet, not all of these people end up becoming alcohol addicts. So the question that begs the most immediate answer is: What makes a person addicted to alcohol?

Of course this is a rather complex question that cannot be answered in simple terms. Nonetheless, experts have identified a number of factors that can cause alcoholism. These are called triggers.

As their name suggests, triggers compel you to feed your addiction. These factors, which may or may not exist independently of each other, influence your attitude and views towards alcohol consumption. As will be later discussed in this book, identifying what your addiction triggers are is important in overcoming your alcohol addiction problem.

## 1. Culture or tradition

Many people belong to cultures where drinking is simply a part of life. Whether it be part of wedding ceremonies, they daily dinner, or sporting events, there are many traditions that we are a part of that demand that we consume alcohol. These cultures can often cause great difficulty in ending alcoholism because they are so engrained in our lives and our relationships with others, and we feel "left out" or alienated if we don't take part in drinking. Culture and tradition is therefore a major trigger for alcohol consumption.

## 2. Domestic triggers

Domestic triggers can be anything related to your family, your finances, and your relationships with the people close to you.

In other words, these are personal issues that you want to run away or escape from. Alcohol may provide a readily available and quick escape. Good examples are when you are having some kind of dispute with your spouse or children, or when you are feeling burdened by debt. These might be just the triggers you need to have a drink to try and forget about things for a while.

3. Psychological triggers

If you are suffering from depression, anxiety, or any other behavioral disorder, then you may be likely to seek refuge in alcohol, which is a perceived guarantee to provide you a temporary way out of your present circumstances. But it is these temporary reprieves from reality that can in and of themselves be addicting. Nursing awful memories of abuse, neglect, and suffering by getting drunk can become cyclical over the long run, and may eventually result in alcohol addiction.

## 4. Environmental factors

Where you grew up and formed your character, as well as your present environment, all play a key role in understanding your alcohol consumption habits. If you came from a household where alcohol consumption was done in a casual manner, then you are likely going to have an equally casual attitude towards drinking. This is particularly true if your parents or any other authority figure exhibited a favorable attitude towards alcohol, in which case you may be more likely to adopt a similar behavior yourself.

This extends to situations outside of the home. If, for instance, you have friends who are heavy drinkers, then you may be more likely to become one too, through association. In other words, who you associate yourself with can have a huge impact on your own worldview, including your regard for alcohol.

## 5. Stress

One of the principal triggers of alcohol addiction is stress. When people are worn out and feel like releasing tension from their system, drinking alcoholic beverages is certainly one of the easier options to take.

It's easy to see how stress, and the consequent need to overcome it, eventually leads to alcohol addiction. When you have poor stress management skills and are inundated by pressure coming from all fronts, alcohol can provide a brief respite as it allows you to relax, loosen up, and temporarily forget about your worries. The experience can be pleasurable, which may be a far cry from the nagging nature of your reality when sober.

## 6. Pain Relief

Some people drink to relieve physical pain that they may experience, either during short-term periods of time, or chronically. Drinking for pain relief may lead to alcoholism if you become dependent on the alcohol. This in turn can lead to further physical problems.

## 7. Biology

For the past few decades, the study of alcohol abuse and dependency has revolved around the assumption that it is a behavioral disorder. However, the result of more recent studies has shown that beyond one's behavior and psychological mindset, biological factors also play a key role in the likeliness that some people will become addicted to alcohol.

Studies conducted by the American Society of Addictions Medicine, for example, yielded the conclusion that one's genetic makeup plays a substantial role (in about 50 percent of cases) to the likeliness that a person is going to become an alcohol addict. This supports an earlier theory suggesting that some people are more predisposed than others to use and abuse alcohol on account of their biological makeup.

The bulk of the research in this field puts a particular emphasis on the brain and how it functions. Alcohol alters the brain's chemical composition and leaves certain "cues" that associate consumption of alcohol with pleasure. Over time these become deeply embedded in one's neurobiological system, and could thereafter be passed on to one's children. This is precisely the reason why a good number of experts are of the opinion that an individual coming from a family with a history of alcohol abuse is likelier than others to develop the same disorder later on in life.

However, one of the criticisms hurled at the idea of alcohol abuse as a gene-based disorder is the fact that it undermines the capacity of individuals to make independent choices for themselves. Since drinking is a deliberate act, it follows that any person who grabs a bottle of alcohol and drinks it down does so of their own will and volition, and not because they are genetically inclined to do so.

In any event, it is generally agreed that more research needs to be done before it can be conclusively held that genes do play a role in the development of an alcohol-related problem. Still, it may be worthwhile noting that if you come from a family background of alcoholism, this may have some bearing on your own alcohol consumption habits.

# Chapter 3: The Effects Of Alcoholism

## In Your Body

As with anything that you do excessively, drinking too much alcohol brings many problems not only when it comes to your social and family life, but more importantly to your health. Alcohol is mainly responsible for many different physical complications that a person can get, especially for those who consume too much.

The body reacts even to the smallest amount of alcohol. Whenever you drink, your body slowly absorbs and circulates it in your bloodstream. Only a very small amount of alcohol leaves your body either through your urinary tract or through your breath. Since your body's absorption of alcohol tends to be slow, its effects can easily be disregarded as long as you eat a lot of food, especially food containing a lot of fat in them. However, if you eat less and you drink more, the chances of you getting drunk become high.

The consumption of alcohol, especially when it is not in moderation, can cause serious problems in the body, and could have adverse effects not only in the mind, but also in other major organ systems. Here are some of the effects that heavy drinking can bring to your body:

The Excretory system. This organ system is responsible for the elimination of waste. When food is digested by the digestive system, some parts are deemed unusable and so are removed through a thorough cleansing process. Being that it is a part of the excretory system, the pancreas produces enzymes that act as digestive juice, which, once combined with bile produced by the gall bladder, help in breaking down food more. In addition to this, the pancreas also helps in the regulation of important bodily chemicals such as insulin and glucose. When a person consumes too much alcohol, the pancreas works on overdrive, and in the process produces very toxic chemicals, which can cause harm to the excretory system and may even go as far as hinder its normal functions. When this happens, the pancreas becomes inflamed, leading to a condition commonly known as pancreatitis. Pancreatitis is a disease, which, if not treated, can destroy the pancreas. Alcohol abuse is commonly cited as the primary cause for having pancreatitis.

Besides the pancreas, another part of the excretory system is the liver. The liver is a big organ made mostly of blood that acts as another part of the body responsible for breaking down substances that can do harm to the body. One of the substances, which are broken down by the liver is alcohol, and when a person consumes too much alcohol, it leads to liver hepatitis, a disease that has obvious symptoms, primarily jaundice or the yellowing of the eyes and the skin. When the liver becomes inflamed due to excessive consumption of alcohol, further complications such as liver cirrhosis can occur. Liver cirrhosis is a condition wherein the liver accumulates scars. When these scars form, they can lead to the destruction and impaired functionality of the liver. When the liver is unable to perform its duties, dangerous substances that are otherwise removed by the liver remain in the body. When these are left inside, they can be life threatening. Women are more at risk of getting alcohol liver diseases than men simply because women's bodies absorb more alcohol yet they process it at a slower pace.

Together, when the liver and the pancreas fail to perform their tasks as excretory system organs, the likelihood of acquiring hypoglycemia, or low blood sugar, rises. When the pancreas is damaged, sugar is not processed due to a lack of insulin. When this happens, hyperglycemia kicks in. This condition is dangerous for those with diabetes. Abuse of alcohol can also lead to liver cancer.

The digestive system. In general, those who drink alcohol heavily can experience trouble absorbing important nutrients from food, especially B vitamins responsible for the maintenance of the immune system and in the control of bacteria entering the body through food. Even with just one incident of heavy drinking, the digestive system can be negatively affected from the mouth to the colon. When a person abuses alcohol, damages are inflicted to the tongue and mouth. The salivary glands become impaired, and this not only affects its tasting capabilities, but it also negatively influences the ability of the mouth to initially digest the food into smaller and more manageable pieces. When saliva is not present to digest food and remove bacteria from the mouth, conditions such as gum disease begin to ensue. In addition, heavy drinking can also be attributed as one of the primary causes for tooth decay and even tooth loss in adults.

Along the lower parts of the digestive tract, abuse of alcohol has been attributed to heartburn, acid reflux, and even to the formation of ulcers in the esophagus. Besides these, inflammation of the stomach and the formation of stomach ulcers can also occur in people who drink heavily. When the digestive system is damaged by excessive drinking, it increases the chances of acquiring stomach, esophagus, throat and mouth cancers. This risk is even more heightened when you are a chronic smoker.

Circulatory system. The heart, all the blood streams of the body, as well as the blood carried through the circulatory system, can be greatly affected by the abuse of alcohol. Your chances of suffering from severe heart conditions rise the more you allow yourself to drink heavily. Some of the complications that you can likely acquire from drinking include: cardiomyopathy or the abnormality of the heart muscles which can lead to difficulty in pumping and in delivering blood to different body parts, arrhythmia or irregularity of heart beats, high blood pressure, heart attack, stroke, and even heart failure. People who have diabetes who drink too much can be at risk of acquiring very low blood sugar levels, and due to the fact that their digestive systems are weaker in absorbing nutrients, they may experience deficiencies in B-vitamins, folic acid, and thiamine, which can consequently negatively affect their blood count, leading to anemia.

The Reproductive system. Excessive alcohol intake negatively affects your sexual and reproductive processes. If you drink too much alcohol, you run the risk of having difficulties in using your reproductive organs not only in sexual intercourse but also in conceiving children. The more you consume alcohol, the more you are damaging your chances of becoming pregnant. Especially if you are one of those people who wish to have children in the future, you are reducing your chances of encouraging pregnancy by drinking too much. Studies have shown that alcohol abuse leads to irregularity in the menstrual cycles, even leading to its sudden halt for extensive periods until it comes to a point when you simply become infertile. As for men, alcohol abuse leads to erectile dysfunctions, as well as in the hindrance in the development and production of important hormones, reducing the quality of the function of the testicles, and eventually leading to infertility.

During pregnancy, a mother who drinks too much becomes at risk of miscarriage. In addition, the likelihood of a stillbirth and a premature delivery increases significantly, especially if the mother drinks through the first and second trimesters. Even when the pregnancy is successful and the child is born at the right time, there are still very big chances that the child has been subjected to complications while it stayed in the womb. Alcohol abuse greatly influences fetal development, especially during the first few weeks of pregnancy when all the major organs and bodily features are first molded into shape. In fact, there is a specific name for the complications brought about by alcoholism to fetal development. These are called FASD's, or Fetal Alcohol Spectrum Disorders. These disorders can range from physical to mental problems at birth. Children who were born out of mothers who drank heavily during pregnancy are more likely to have abnormalities physically, as well as have difficulties in learning and in handling their emotions. These problems will last their entire lifetimes.

The Muscular and Skeletal Systems. Alcohol abuse negatively affects the production of new bones and muscles. In the case of the skeletal system, alcohol abuse causes a complete stop in the production of new bones. The quality of existing ones become poor too, and can lead to fractures and osteoporosis in the future. On the other hand, people who drink too much also run the risk of being prone to muscle cramps, overall weakness, and even muscle atrophy.

The Central Nervous System. Alcohol, as is known to many people, makes people prone to not thinking things through and subjects them to hallucinations and confusion. Alcohol dulls a person's thinking.

Alcohol travels very, very fast throughout the body, and it can reach many different parts of your body in seconds, with your central nervous system being one of those places. Alcohol makes it difficult for you to clearly speak, making your pronunciation of words slow and slurred. This, obviously, is one of the sure signs that a person is already drunk. Alcohol also affects your motor skills as well as your sense of balance, which makes it difficult to walk a straight line when you are drunk.

Abusive use of alcohol leads to difficulty in thinking clearly, as well as hindering your capabilities to act on impulse and to form new memories. After a long period of heavy drinking, the frontal lobes of the brain responsible for sound decision-making and consideration of consequence for actions done, literally shrink in size. This can lead to delirium and to episodic seizures. If alcoholism ensues, it leads to permanent brain damage, going as far as dementia.

When alcohol abuse damages the nervous system, it can lead to abnormal sensations of pain and numbness in the extremities such as the hands and feet. Thiamine or

Vitamin B1 deficiency, brought by excessive amounts of alcohol in the body for prolonged periods of time, results in weakness, eye muscle paralysis, and even involuntary rapid eye movements.

The Immune system. This part of the body is responsible for protecting you from foreign substances that may harbor with them certain bacteria or viruses that can either make you ill or kill you. The body is protected by many types of cells under the immune system, from white blood cells that run through the blood stream, to antibodies that linger in organs and eat up viruses when they see them. However, if you drink too much, you are reducing the ability of the immune system of properly doing its job. When the immune system fails to do its job, various types of viruses enter the body and cause havoc, leading to multiple illnesses and complications. Abusive drinkers are more likely to develop tuberculosis and pneumonia than the rest of the population. Besides these, drinking too much can greatly increase the risk of accumulating different variations of cancer.

# Chapter 4: Why Do People Drink?

Neurological Effects of Alcohol

In this section, let us look at the neurological effects of alcohol consumption that might prompt you to drink alcohol.

It is rather surprising that a seemingly simple molecule such as alcohol can have extremely complicated effects. It's a popular belief that alcohol helps reduce stress, albeit temporarily, and a lot of people resort to drinking alcohol for this purpose. Alcohol increases the uptake of a neurotransmitter known as GABA (gamma-aminobutyric acid), which helps reduce stress. It is believed to be the brain's primary inhibitor. Whenever GABA molecules start increasing in the brain, the overall effect is quite similar to the one you might experience when you take any tranquilizers, such as Valium or Xanax. However, GABA is not the only neurotransmitter that alcohol influences, but there are other neurotransmitters too. When the GABA molecules increase, it reduces your brain's uptake of glutamate, which is an excitatory molecule. It might sound like it results in more inhibition and less excitation. Well, this is an oversimplification of the neurological effects of alcohol consumption.

Your prefrontal cortex regulates your ability to think and plan. Whenever you consume alcohol, the functioning of the prefrontal cortex tends to get inhibited. It is one of the reasons why people associate poor and flawed decision making with the consumption of alcohol. Whenever you start drinking alcohol, your ability to view things rationally reduces, and your ability to think from any other perspective other than your own becomes nonexistent. A noteworthy side effect of this overall dimming in your thought process might make you believe that your thoughts become extremely clear. You might also start to revel in this feeling. However, it only means that your thinking has become limited.

While this happens, GABA starts to slowly remove all breaks to the system that produces dopamine in your body. Dopamine is a feel-good hormone that prompts feelings of pleasure and reward. When excessive dopamine is produced, it tempts your brain to retrace its steps and indulge in the same behaviors that helped produce the exciting pleasures and rewards you previously enjoyed. So, what happens when GABA lets go of all brakes on the production of dopamine? What will happen if you let go of the brakes in a car? The car will move ahead. When dopamine starts flooding your system, your brain ignites the desire for a specific reward, such as feeling less stressed and more happy. Then comes anticipation (bringing the glass to your lips and drinking), which is finally followed by a reward (feeling good).

So, consuming alcohol tends to relax you physically. It, in turn, reduces stress and judgment. Therefore, it becomes easier to talk to others and behave as you want to. Apart from all this, it also starts initiating your brain's reward system that makes you anticipate something good is about to happen. There is another neurotransmitter that steps into the picture whenever you consume alcohol. This neurotransmitter is an opioid. No, opioids are not necessarily found in drugs, but even your body releases internal opiates known as endorphins. Endorphins are feel-good hormones, and they are released whenever you consume alcohol. We are all aware that opiates make us feel good, but we can get the desired dose of opiate legally by drinking a stiff drink. For instance, the American martini includes 3 ounces of gin. The faster you consume this alcohol, the more opiates your body releases and hence the feel-good effect.

When you start considering all the aspects of an alcohol high, it isn't surprising that inebriation feels quite different to different individuals. This feeling also shifts dramatically from the first of the last drink of the night. It becomes a little difficult, especially when it is hard to stop. All those who are bogged down by stress consume alcohol to relax. All those who work hard on resisting them, pulses drink to let go of their impulses. The first drink of the night is quite exciting, and the last drink has an almost sedative effect.

For instance, an underage adult indulging in binge drinking is consuming all the chemicals in the alcohol to alter his mood to make himself feel better. If they keep at it for another 20 years, he will probably start drinking to feel less instead of more because life is riddled with anxieties and stress. However, once an individual is addicted to alcohol, the main reason why he keeps drinking is definitely not for the fun quotient. Two primary fears make an individual addicted to alcohol. The first reason is the fear of not drinking, and the second reason is the fear of an inability to stop drinking. The one thing no one realizes about drinking is that the source of their relaxation is also the source of their stress. It can be tricky to find a way out of a vicious cycle of anxiety, coupled with temporary relief. However, you can break free of this cycle using the information given in the subsequent chapters.

Common Reasons

Motivation is the inherent desire that fuels us to work toward our goals. Do you know where motivation stems from? It stems from wishing to experience the benefits of attaining a goal. Two factors influence your levels of motivation, and they are the value of pursuing a goal and the success you can attain by achieving the goals. So, your commitment is strengthened and dependent on the perceived value and the chances of the value coming true. Therefore, it is obvious that the relationship between these factors is multiplication. It essentially means you would have no motivation to pursue a goal if the value associated with it is zero, regardless of your chances of success. Likewise, if the chances of success are quite low, you will have no motivation to pursue the goal.

The goal of consuming alcohol is pretty much formed the same way as with any other goals. It is primarily determined by the value that someone associates with alcohol and their chances of attaining the desired outcome. So, the decision to drink is determined largely by the value you attribute to drinking alcohol and the chances of attaining that outcome. Perhaps it is to improve your level of confidence, overcome anxiety, let go of a negative mood, or just to feel better.

In this section, let us carefully consider the common factors that prompt an individual's desire to consume alcohol.

Stress Relief

After a stressful day, you might feel the urge to have a stiff drink. It could be your idea of relaxation. Well, as mentioned in the previous section, alcohol consumption does produce certain feel-good hormones in your body. All those experiencing extreme stress or going through a stressful period in life resort to drinking because it helps reduce the negative feelings they experience. They start associating a great value with drinking and start consuming more alcohol since it helps alleviate some of their anxiety. However, stress relief is only temporary. Once the effect of alcohol fades away, the stress will be back.

Overall Environment

Your environment tends to affect you, and you might not even realize it. Being exposed to an environment filled with alcohol-related cues can easily trigger your craving for alcohol. For instance, advertisements, TV shows, or even movies that glorify drinking can tempt you to drink. You might start thinking that, "If someone on screen can look cool by drinking, then so can I."

Peer Pressure and Camaraderie

A lot of people drink because those around them drink. So, they start believing that if they don't drink, they will not fit in with the group. In a way, they are experiencing indirect peer pressure to drink so that they are not left out. For instance, someone might feel that he is obligated to drink whenever his co-workers are going for a drink at happy hour. This is an instance of indirect peer pressure. However, peer pressure can be more direct and stronger. For instance, if you're out with your group of friends, and they start actively encouraging you to drink, it becomes quite difficult to say no. You might start feeling like you cannot hang out with them if you don't drink. So, you go ahead and drink. It all boils down to the way you start viewing camaraderie in your mind. It can become quite difficult to say no to alcohol, especially when someone starts pushing you to consume it. It can become even more difficult for a young adult, especially when he is ridiculed for not drinking alcohol.

Accessibility

Another common reason why people drink is that they can drink. They might or might not want to drink, but merely because they can drink, they start drinking. This reason might not make any sense, but think about it for a moment. If you live in an area where you have absolutely no access to alcohol, then your chances of drinking will reduce. On the other hand, if you live somewhere where alcohol is readily available, the chances of you drinking will increase.

Mental Condition

A common reason why individuals who suffer from a drinking problem is that they have an unidentified underlying mental health condition. They start using alcohol as a means to self-soothe and self-medicate. If this condition isn't diagnosed, they might be consuming alcohol to reduce the symptoms of their mental health condition unknowingly. Common underlying mental health conditions that lead to excessive drinking are social anxiety, obsessive-compulsive disorder, bipolar disorder, anxiety, depression, post-traumatic stress disorder, schizophrenia, and a history of abuse. Whenever such people start drinking, they might feel quite euphoric and revel in its relaxing effect. All these effects help alleviate stress or temporarily escape the problem they might be facing.

Let Go of Inhibitions

We all have specific personality traits that shape the way we are. These traits also influence how others perceive us. Some people resort to drinking alcohol because it allows them to let go of their inhibitions. Once you drop these inhibitions, your overall behavior changes. So, it isn't surprising that people drink alcohol to allow others to perceive them differently. For instance, a tomboy might admire the fact that men easily engage in risky behavior after they start drinking. So, she might start drinking to show that she can be as cool and careless as a man. Or a man who is trying to gain a woman's attention might start drinking to let go of his inhibitions, which are preventing him from gaining attention. After downing a couple of drinks, he might realize that all the doubts and worries he had slowly fade away. In both these instances, people are drinking merely to let go of their inhibitions. So, people drink because they want to create a new identity that forces others to see them the way they want to be seen.

Past Experiences

Your past experiences with drinking alcohol can also shape your present relationship with it. For instance, if you had fun after drinking alcohol or have certain fond memories associated with the consumption of alcohol, you will naturally be more inclined to drink again. On the other hand, if you had a bad experience or experienced alcohol flush (nausea and headaches) after drinking, you wouldn't be that keen to drink.

Impulsive Personality

All those individuals who are considered to be impulsive usually opt for immediate rewards. Therefore, they don't see any harm in engaging in certain acts as long as they get an immediate result. They do this even if it has negative repercussions in the long run. So, they start placing excessive value on the consumption of alcohol because of its rewarding nature. It is one of the reasons why heavy drinkers are usually more impulsive than light drinkers. In fact, it reaches a stage where they love their impulsive nature.

## Social Norms

Regardless of what you might want to believe, societal norms can be quite stressful. Social norms are the expected set of behaviors within a specific community. Social norms affect and shape the value individuals associate with alcohol consumption. For instance, in most of the western societies, consumption of alcohol is associated with specific events and at regular times. It could be in the form of drinking every Friday night after successfully completing a week at work. Or maybe a casual drink before going to bed at night. To an extent, these norms might limit and control the consumption of alcohol. However, when left unchecked, an individual might end up developing a drinking problem without even realizing it. If you start drinking every Friday night and then miss one drinking night, you might feel a little odd. Societal norms condition the mind and encourage the development of certain habits.

Rebellion

Some people start drinking because they see it as a form of rebellion. This stands especially true in a young crowd. Such individuals believe that they are defying rules to show that they are quite different from those around them. This act of rebellion might also make an adolescent, or a teen, feel quite good and powerful. It is basic human nature to try and defy rules. For instance, when someone asks you not to do something, the urge to do it will increase. This logic stands true for drinking, especially when young adults are repeatedly told not to drink.

For Fun

People like to drink alcohol since they think they have more fun when they consume alcohol. Whenever they are drinking, they might experience feelings that are quite similar to being happy or even spirited. Drinking with your friends can be an exciting experience. If an individual is nervous in social settings, then drinking might help let go of his inhibitions and have more fun. It is one of the reasons why people drink a lot at parties, barbecues, nightclubs, or any other social setting. They do this because they believe that alcohol helps elevate their overall experience.

Mood Regulation

Drinking to improve one's mood might not sound like a bad idea. If you can improve your mood by having a couple of drinks, then what is the harm? Plenty of people drink because they believe that something is entirely wrong with their mood, and alcohol offers an escape. It gives you the respite that you require to tolerate the state you are in, which makes dealing with a negative mood quite better.

Curiosity

Curiosity is a common reason that is associated with a younger crowd. Teens, college students, and at times, even preteens start drinking because they are curious about what it tastes like and what it would feel like to be drunk. Their curiosity tends to get the better of them. They might start experimentally consuming alcohol. They do this to merely get the sense of what it would feel like to have firsthand experience. However, when left unchecked, this kind of behavior can quickly escalate into a drinking problem.

## Resistance

When you start exercising, you might initially be able to run for half a mile without breaking a sweat. If you keep exercising regularly, you will reach a point where you can run two miles without breaking a sweat. Why does this happen? It happens because your body starts getting accustomed to the idea of exercising and slowly develops resistance. The same logic applies to alcohol.

Whenever you consume alcohol, it gives you a pleasant high. It is one of the reasons why people even start drinking in the first place. However, your body tends to become more resistant as you keep drinking more alcohol. Therefore, it takes more alcohol to get the desired buzz. For instance, you probably used to get a buzz after a martini. After a while, you might have realized that you need three martinis to get the same buzz. It is because your body is slowly developing resistance to the effects of alcohol. When you keep doing the same thing repeatedly, you develop immunity to it. So, you might be able to drink more without experiencing any of the negative effects of alcohol. Since you don't get drunk, you or others around you might unknowingly assume that you don't have a problem. It is one of the most hazardous forms of alcoholism because by the time anyone realizes, the damage might be done.

Regardless of why you drink, understand that there is a difference between casual and abusive drinking. It simply means that some people are incapable of drinking at a normal rate. When left unregulated, this habit can quickly turn into an obsession.

You must understand these factors because they are the primary reasons why you drink. If you want to stop drinking, you cannot do this unless you understand your primary motivation. Once you identify them, it becomes easier to find alternate sources to derive the perceived value you associate with drinking. For instance, if your primary motivation to drink is to feel more included in your peer group, then you can come up with alternate ways to achieve this objective without consuming alcohol. Perhaps you can start engaging in lively conversations or meeting them more often. You will learn about how to stop drinking in the subsequent chapters.

## Chapter 5: Alcohol: The Root Cause

## Of Many Social Problems

Alcohol is not only detrimental to your health; it slowly changes you and your life like poison. It changes people's behavior and makes them either aggressive or hopeless. It is also one of the major causes of death among young people. Other bad habits also start developing, such as gambling, lust, disregard for relationships and people also start losing the sense of right and wrong. That is why alcohol plays a major part in the increasing crime rates. So it is important to look into certain facts and figures that point to the social horrors of alcohol abuse because you don't want to wake up one day with the realization that you cannot make amends for what you have done. Stop and think before you are going to pour yourself another drink because it's not only a matter of your life; it's also a matter of the lives of the people around you.

It's Lethal

It is alarming to note that alcohol kills more young people than all other drugs combined. Due to the consumption of alcohol, there has been an increase in the number of young people being killed between the ages of 14 to 25, in accidents, suicides and homicides. According to a survey in 2007, 12, 998 people were killed in alcohol related traffic accidents in the U.S. In England, there is approximately a 7% increase in alcohol related deaths every year. All over the world, at least 40-50% of the traffic deaths involve alcohol. So, alcoholics not only harm themselves intentionally or unintentionally, they also harm others. This teaches us to be cautious and not to make alcohol a part of our lives because you never know whether or not you can limit the amount you drink. You might start with one drink a day but later on you get dependent on it and you become a number in these statistics. That is what you should dread and you should try to fight against alcohol consumption because your life is too precious to be wasted like that.

Increasing Crime Rates

It is an undeniable fact that alcohol is the leading cause of increased crime rates. A study conducted by the US Department of Justice shows that 40% of violent crimes are committed under the influence of alcohol. Murder, street crimes, violent fights, rape, illegal drug usage, and domestic violence and abuse show a horrible picture of alcohol consumption. That is why it is important to stay away from it and to keep an eye on your children because teenagers easily fall prey to these dangers. If children start to drink from teenage, 32% of them also start using illegal drugs. Alcohol slowly tarnishes people's personalities and their characters. It starts with bad language and disrespect for relationships and simple rules, then lead to aggressive behavior and finally violent crimes.

Financial Problems

Once you start drinking, you can become dependent on it quickly. That dependence costs a lot of money, especially if you are a binge drinker. Heavy drinking also affects your performance at work. Sometimes, people lose their jobs because they are sleepy at work, show clear signs of having a hangover or they make a lot of mistakes. People who regularly drink are more likely to waste money on gambling and prostitutes. Many people also lose their established business and reputation due to alcohol consumption. Mostly, alcoholics incur debts which prove to be a huge blow for the family and affect their children very badly. If you are facing a financial crisis because of alcohol addiction, then it's time for you to get help. Stop drinking alcohol and live life to its full extent.

Family Problems

A lot of the time, alcohol consumption also leads to family problems. This habit creates a gap between you and your family because you don't give them enough time. Sometimes, it becomes the cause of frequent fights and shouting. Those who have children, damage their minds with these quarrels without even knowing it. When kids see their parents fighting, it either embeds fear in their minds or they become angry and violent. Often, drunken parents abuse their children. This domestic violence and abuse can tear the families apart. In most of the cases, parents get separated, leaving their children in a state of agony. You don't want your family to be like that. You don't want to doom yourself and your loved ones to this fate.

To avoid all these issues, make a resolution of not drinking alcohol and keep it, not only for your sake, but also for the sake of your loved ones. You cannot change the past but you can control what you are going to do now and change the future. Just relax, go to someplace quiet and think about the outcomes of your choices. That is how you can change your life and open up better avenues for yourself.

# Chapter 6: Negatives of

# Alcohol/Why You Should Quit

There are most likely more than a million and one reasons why you should want to quit drinking, especially if you are a heavy drinker and/or have an addiction to alcoholic beverages. Some of the most important of these reasons have to do with your health. Hangovers alone are an uncomfortable and unhealthy side effect of heavy alcohol consumption and of course, alcohol poisoning, but those are just 2 of some of the most well-known negative consequences you can suffer from when you abuse alcohol. But alcohol addiction can affect your health in a lot of other very negative ways as well, and some of these negative effects have the potential to become life-threatening.

Alcohol Poisoning

Alcohol poisoning is much worse than any hangover, and the symptoms can range from moderate to severe. The most extreme and severe cases of alcohol poisoning can be life-threatening. The signs and symptoms of alcohol poisoning can include:

Disorientation and confusion

Pale-looking skin (sometimes with a bluish tinge)

Hypothermia (a drop in body temperature)

Stupor (unresponsiveness while still conscious)

Passing out

Unusual breathing rhythm

Very slow and/or labored breathing

Vomiting

In some of the more extreme cases of alcohol poisoning, your breathing may even stop completely. You could also suffer a heart attack, choke on your own vomit, and/or vomit may be inhaled into your lungs which can also cause life-threatening damage. The symptoms of hypothermia can also become dangerous. Also, if you lose too much fluid and suffer severe dehydration, you can put yourself at risk for brain damage. And, if your blood glucose levels drop too low, you can suffer from seizures.

If you suffer from a case of alcohol poisoning serious enough, you can even risk going into a coma and eventually dying.

The Effects of Alcohol on Your Liver

Alcohol can be harmful to a number of different organs in your body, and one of the organs it can be especially harmful to your liver. Your liver is a part of the human body that regularly works overtime. It's the largest internal organ in your body and it has about 500 separate functions. One of the most important jobs that your liver does is breaking down food and then converting that food into energy. Additionally, your liver aids in ridding your body of waste products. It also plays an imperative part when it comes to fighting certain infections, especially those that can occur in the bowel.

If your liver does become damaged, you usually will not even realize it until the damage begins to cause serious problems. Heavy drinking increases your risk of liver disease and can also cause irreparable damage to your liver. There are many different causes of liver disease, and heavy drinking can cause what is known as: "alcoholic liver disease."

Oxidative stress- When your liver attempts its break down process on alcohol, the chemical reaction that results can be damaging to its cells. The damage can cause your liver to become inflamed and scared from trying to repair itself.

Toxins in gut bacteria- Alcohol can also cause damage your intestine. Your intestine allows the toxins from your gut bacteria to enter your liver. These toxins can also cause the same type of inflammation and scarring.

Excessive drinking can also cause your liver to become fat. (Quitting drinking can help it shrink back down to its normal size)This is a condition called "fatty liver" or "steatosis." Your liver transforms glucose into fat and then sends it all over your body to be stored for when it is needed.

Alcohol negatively affects the way your liver processes fat and causes your liver's cells to fill with it. If this happens to you, you may start to feel some type of discomfort in your abdomen area due to your liver being swollen. You may also begin to feel sick and start losing your appetite. If you don't stop drinking, your fatty liver condition will worsen and eventually develop into the next stage of liver disease.

You can spend over 20 years damaging your liver and not feel the effects. Early symptoms of liver disease can include:

Fatigue

Nausea

Vomiting

Diarrhea

Abdominal pains

In the later stages of liver damage, your symptoms began to get more serious, and you will feel them. These are the symptoms of liver conditions called "alcoholic hepatitis" and/or "fibrosis." The symptoms can include:

Jaundice (yellowing of your skin)

Vomiting up blood

Fatigue (moderate to severe)

Weakness and loss of appetite

Itching skin

Easy bruising

Swelling of your legs ankles, and/or abdomen

Liver cancer

Bleeding in your gut

Increased sensitivity to alcohol and drugs (both medical drugs and recreational drugs)

Your liver being unable to process any type of drugs

Cirrhosis of the liver

Alcohol can cause you to develop cirrhosis, and quitting alcohol is vital to keep you from dying of liver failure. Liver failure is when your liver completely stops working.

In the most severe cirrhosis cases, the only way to be considered for a liver transplant is if you stop drinking alcohol for at least 3 months. If you stop soon enough, you can actually reverse the liver problems caused by alcohol. Once you develop cirrhosis, your prognosis is going to partly depend on whether or not you quit drinking. If you do continue to drink, you will increase your risk for those with symptoms of dying from liver failure.

The Effects of Alcohol on Your Brain

Heavy alcohol drinking can throw the balance of neurotransmitters off its course. Alcohol can cause the neurotransmitters in your brain to relay information much too slowly, which can cause you to feel extremely drowsy.

Alcohol--caused neurotransmitter balance can trigger mood and behavioral changes. These can include:

Depression

Agitation

Memory loss

Seizures

Long -term heavy drinking will cause alterations in the brain's neurons, like brain cell size reductions. As a result, your brain mass ends up shrinking and the inner cavity of your brain grows larger. These changes can actually affect a wide array of your abilities, including things like:

Motor coordination

Temperature regulation

Sleeping patterns

Mood

A variety of cognitive functions- including your learning skills and memory skills.

One of the neurotransmitters in your brain particularly susceptible—even to small amounts of alcohol—is your glutamate. Your glutamate affects other things in your body, but none so much as memory. Researchers feel that alcohol interferes with the actions of your glutamates, and this is most likely what causes some individuals to temporarily "black out," and/or forget what happened on a night where they were engaged in heavy drinking.

Alcohol can also cause an increase in your brain's release of serotonin, which is another neurotransmitter that helps regulate your emotional expression and endorphins. Endorphins are natural substances that can ignite feelings of relaxation and/or euphoria as alcoholic intoxication sets in. Researchers now know that the brain attempts to compensate for all of these disruptions. The neurotransmitters adapt in order to create balance in your brain despite fact that alcohol is present. But having to make these adaptations can also end up creating negative results. These results can include building alcohol tolerance, developing alcohol dependence, and experiencing symptoms of alcohol withdrawal.

The Effects of Alcohol on Your Heart

Drinking alcohol can also cause damage to your heart. These problems can include:

Cardiomyopathy (Stretching and/or drooping of your heart muscles)

Arrhythmias (an irregular heartbeat)

Stroke

High blood pressure

The Effects of Alcohol on Your Pancreas

Alcohol can cause your pancreas to produce toxic substances. These toxins can gradually lead to a condition called pancreatitis. The symptoms of pancreatitis include dangerous inflammation and swelling of your pancreas' blood vessels which prevents proper digestion. Pancreatic damage can cause your body to not have the ability to utilize sugar because of its lack of insulin. This can lead to a condition called "hyperglycemia." Blood sugar levels that become unbalanced can be a potentially dangerous problem—especially for those individuals who are already suffering from diabetes.

## The Effects of Alcohol on Your Bodily Systems

### Central Nervous System

Alcohol easily travels throughout your body, and can quickly reach many areas of your body. These areas include your brain as well as other important parts of your body's central nervous system. This can make it harder for you to talk, which causes slurring of your speech—one of the telltale signs that a person has consumed too much alcohol. This can also have a negative affect your coordination as well as interfere with your balance and you ability to walk properly.

Drinking too much alcohol negatively affects your ability to think clearly. It also affects your impulse control and your ability to form memories. The long-term affects can actually cause the frontal lobes of your brain to shrink. Acute alcoholic withdrawal symptoms can cause seizures as well as delirium. It can also progress to permanent brain damage which in turn, causes dementia.

Damaging your nervous system can cause numbness, pain, and/or abnormal sensations in your hands and feet. Alcoholism can cause a deficiency in thiamine (vitamin B1). This can result in involuntary rapid eye movement as well as weakness and/or paralysis of your eye muscles.

Men and women metabolize alcohol differently. It generally takes less alcohol to affect women.

Over time, a heavy drinker can become physically and emotionally dependent on alcohol. It may be very difficult to gain control. Unlike most other common addictions, acute alcohol withdrawal can be life threatening. Cases of severe, chronic alcohol addiction often require medical

Digestive System

Alcohol can have a huge negative impact on every part of your digestive system—starting from your mouth and continuing all the way to your colon.

Abusing alcohol can damage your salivary glands and also irritate your mouth and tongue. This can lead to tooth decay, gum disease, and even loss of your teeth. Heavy drinking can also cause you to develop ulcers in your esophagus, heartburn and/or acid reflux. Also, stomach ulcers and the inflammation of your stomach lining (a condition called gastritis) can occur.

Inflammation of your pancreas will interfere with its ability to aid in the digestive process and regulate your body's metabolism. Damaging your digestive system can cause abdominal fullness, gassiness and diarrhea. It can lead to dangerous internal bleeding that can be due to hemorrhoids, ulcers or esophageal varices caused by cirrhosis.

Alcohol can make it much more difficult for your digestive tract to absorb B vitamins and nutrients and/or control bacteria. Heavy drinkers usually suffer from malnutrition, and they also face having a higher risk of developing cancer of the mouth, throat, esophagus and/or colon.

Circulatory System

Alcohol can cause the following circulatory system complications:

Poisoning of the heart muscle cells (cardiomyopathy)

Irregular heartbeat (arrhythmia)

High blood pressure

Stroke

Heart attack

Heart failure

Individuals who are diabetic have an increased risk of developing low blood sugar levels—especially if they are insulin users. Vitamins B6, B12, thiamine, and folic acid deficiencies can lead to a drop in blood counts. One of the most common symptoms of anemia is fatigue.

## Reproductive System

A common side effect of alcohol abuse in men is erectile dysfunction. It can also cause the inhibition of hormone production, affect testicular functions, and even cause infertility.

Heavy alcohol consumption can make women stop menstruating and cause them to become infertile. It also can increase a pregnant woman's risk of miscarriage, premature delivery, and/or stillbirth.

Alcohol can have an extremely negative effect on a fetus's development. A wide array of developmental problems called "fetal alcohol spectrum disorders" or (FASD) can occur. The symptoms of FASD can include physical abnormalities, emotional issues and learning difficulties that can last an entire lifetime. In women, the risk of developing breast cancer also increases with heavy alcohol use.

## Skeletal and Muscle Systems

Long-term alcohol abuse will make it more difficult for your body to create and produce new bone. Heavy drinking increases your risk of developing osteoporosis, which is the thinning of your bones, and bone fractures. Your body's muscles also become more prone to weakness, cramping, and even atrophy.

Immune System

When your immune system is weakened by heavy alcohol consumption, it has a difficult time being able to fight off germs, viruses, and virtually any type of illness. Alcoholics are much more likely to develop pneumonia or tuberculosis than the rest of the general population. Alcohol abuse also increases your risk of developing many different forms of cancer.

Sounds pretty bad doesn't it? These are enough reason to make you want to seriously consider giving up alcohol, and the truth of the matter is—it really is never "too late" to quit drinking alcohol, even if you are already suffering from alcohol cirrhosis or other serious medical conditions.

The Detoxification Process

When an alcoholic stops drinking abruptly, they're likely to experience symptoms of withdrawal, such as:

Nausea

Anxiety

Nervousness

Tremors

In some of the more severe cases, your symptoms can lead to confusion, hallucinations (also called: delirium tremens), and even seizures. Alcohol detoxification can usually take somewhere between 2 to 7 days. If your withdrawal symptoms become very bothersome or severe, there are certain medications your doctor can prescribe for you which can help prevent them and/or make them a lot more manageable.

## Chapter 7: Why You Drink More

## Than You Want To

You wake up. You feel rubbish. How much did you drink last night? Can't recall exactly? The only thing you're sure of is that it was much more than you expected it to be. Again.

Then, why does this propensity to drink too much exist? Is it just that you get carried away at the moment and lose count?

Or that you're weak-willed and can't just say no? Is it just you? Is something wrong with you? Isn't this a symptom of alcoholism?

There are two very clear reasons why people tend to drink too much and feel that they have to exercise the willpower to control what they drink, and both reasons apply to all. You should be assured that you are not wrong about anything, and it does not necessarily mean that you are an alcoholic! The first reason is to deal with the varying time it takes to run its course with two unique effects of alcohol; mental stimulation and physical intoxication. The second has to do with the physiological response of the body to alcohol. Let's all recognize them in sequence.

Physical Intoxication vs. Mental Relaxation
The most common reason people reach for a drink is for the comforting, relaxing effect. Alcohol is an anesthetic; it 11

ALCOHOLEXPLAINED

anesthetizes certain emotions (such as exhaustion, tension, pain, and discomfort), and the result of this is that, after a drink, we appear to feel more mentally comfortable. Of course, the depressive/anesthetic effects not only work on our mind; they also affect the rest of our body, making us slightly uncoordinated and slow. This is the effect of one or two drinks; we increase the effects on both sides if we increase our consumption, resulting in full-blown intoxication.

The calming mental effect and the physical disability or intoxication have often been believed to go hand in hand and parcel of the same process. This is not the case, however. The mental relaxation and physical intoxication run their course at different speeds.

To give an instance of this, where many people face drinking-driving laws, they can be over the limit while driving the next morning after a night of heavy drinking. Processing one unit of alcohol (a unit being around half a pint of beer or a single measure of spirits) takes the average person one hour, so you can easily see how you might be over the limit for driving the next day, particularly if you drank a lot the night before and if you live in a country with a zero-tolerance law (i.e., where you are not allowed to have alcohol in your system while driving).

However, the vast majority of individuals caught drink driving the next day do not feel drunk, which is why it is an area of concern. They honestly believe they are sober. It is just those who have not been drinking for a long time or those who normally drink modest quantities and then have a big binge, who still feel intoxicated the next morning. This is because their bodies have not yet learned to fight the amount of alcohol that has been consumed effectively. The morning after drinking, people who still have alcohol in their bloodstream will 12

13

ALCOHOLEXPLAINED

Take another drink. But even though the calming effect has worn off, the intoxication hasn't, so now you are comfortable with one drink but intoxicated with two drinks. The calming effect soon wears off again, and the feeling of nervousness resurfaces, so you drink another drink. Now you're three intoxicated but still one relaxed. Just as the evening wears on the intoxication, as you try to pursue the feeling of comfort, it keeps growing.

This is how we can wake up the morning after a heavy night and still be physically intoxicated even if the calming effects of the drink are long gone. This is also why almost every drinker who has ever existed has had at least one instance when too much alcohol has been ingested unintentionally. In fact, almost every single drinker has consumed too much alcohol on occasion, but on many occasions, the vast majority have done so and continue to do so throughout their drinking lives.

Drinkers have to be careful of drinking too much. Are they having the same coffee, water, tea, or soft drink problems? It is commonplace for their partner to give an alert about drinking too much if a husband or wife goes out for a drink one evening, but if the person goes out for a coffee, do they ever get told, "Just make sure you don't have too much, you know you get really shaky and can't sleep when you have too much caffeine"?

# Chapter 8: Change The Way You

# Think

In any type of problem, the first step is to acknowledge what is presently happening, and to accept what the person has done and what is being done as of the moment. They have to admit that they have currently wronged the use of alcohol and have instead, abused the use of it, which led to alcohol abuse and addiction. People have to acknowledge and accept first what they have done in the past so that they would have the clarity of mind to see where they are currently standing and what has happened to them because of that thing that was done. There has to be the initiative to see where they currently are, and to have the conviction to be where they should be or to do what they should rightfully do. Without this initiative, there will be no desire to see the present, which would prevent them from seeing their future prospect, in connection to their abuse of alcohol intake. The first step therefore, is to create a purpose by means of rational thought, to understand that by abusing the intake of alcohol they have committed a mistake, which they should alter because it is not good and not healthy for them. As one expert in this subject have said, a person will eventually lead to nowhere if he or she is denial about it, minimizing it and belittling it like it is not one of the most important things that had to be refurbished in life.

Once a person has entered into rational thought, it is time to acknowledge a purpose. They should try to think why they should do it, why they should drink tons of alcohol for an unlimited time. What is the purpose or the objective for that act that they are doing? Is there something good that they would profit out of drinking too much alcohol over a period of time? Are there some benefits? What are they? They should try and meditate over the act of alcohol intake that they are presently experiencing, and see what the advantages the action brings to them as a person. This is the time for meditation, when the person begins to ask about the main purpose the action is being subjected to. They have to realize that they do not just drink because they are thirsty, but because of the effect of anxiety, depression, as well as pain. They are looking for something that would numb them from these negative emotions, and they have found the answer in a bottle of alcohol. Once they have acknowledged these things, it will be clear why they are doing it and what they really want to do, whether they want to continue doing it or maybe one day stop doing it. The purpose will become more evident, as they are able to understand more their reason for doing it.

After the person has acknowledged the purpose, it is then time to create a mission that is: to try and stop alcohol addiction once and for all. They have to choose to overcome alcohol addiction. No one will push them to stop alcohol addiction. It is up to them to choose whether they want to continue or if they want to stop it. They have to understand that what happens to them is everything that they have wanted to happen to them. No one else can tell them to do this or to engage in this; to stop this or to give this up. Even if all their relatives and friends are there to support them as they give up alcohol addiction, everything and everyone will be useless unless the person decides to stop it themselves, to do it themselves. If they do not choose to do it, then nobody can do it for them. Thus, they have to choose to overcome alcohol addiction. They have to see why they have to stop this abuse of alcohol intake, and what leads them to become, as a result of alcohol abuse and addiction. As it is said, the biggest leverage in the lives of people can be found in the hearts and in the minds. There is nobody who can eliminate these things from their lives but them and only them.

Meanwhile, it is important to think that, what people intend to become they will soon become. It is important to experience the theory of expectancy, wherein people develop the belief that,what they want to become, they will soon become. They have to believe that if they want to stop alcohol abuse and addiction, then time will come when they will finally see these things as events of the past. There will no longer be alcoholism in their lives but only the courage to take what is only necessary— just enough for the time being, enough for the body, enough for the mind. If people have certain expectancy with regards to their initiative, then that objective will become easier to handle, no matter how difficult it is for the time being. In time, they will get motivated to continue doing what they feel they should do, as they can visualize themselves in light, wherein they successfully get over their difficulties in life, especially when it comes to alcoholism. The first step therefore, is to tune in their thoughts and their minds, to make sure that they are concentrated on accomplishing their task, no matter how difficult it seemed.

# Chapter 9: Dangers To Watch Out For

It is very important that you prepare yourself for your alcohol fast. Not too many people can quit cold-turkey and it is wise to be informed and have a plan. We will present an action plan later in this book, but first, let's see what you might expect to happen

Danger Signs Of Alcohol Detoxification

You may think you are not addicted to alcohol because you only drink on weekends or have a drink once or twice a day. Your body may have other ideas about this and it is very important that you pay attention to what your body is doing during your alcohol fast. Alcohol withdrawal symptoms range from the moderate to life-threateningly severe; they can accelerate quickly with possibly deadly consequences.

Literally, alcohol withdrawal has the potential to kill you. Everyone is different; while one individual can get away with a drink a day and not be physically dependant on alcohol, another person might not be so lucky. This is why you must really pay attention to what your body is telling you for six to 48 hours after you take your last drink.

I would suggest that you do not do this alone. Have someone you trust nearby for this critical period and educate them with what might occur and how to handle it.

Social Drinker Vs. Addiction

I always thought myself to be a social drinker and assumed I could take it or leave it. Addiction is insidious because it sneaks up on you. That is why this month-long fast from alcohol is important. If you truly are just a social drinker, you should experience few to no effects from alcohol detox. However, if you have become addicted to alcohol, the effects of withdrawing "cold turkey" will be much more dramatic. Symptoms start out mild but grow in intensity, eventually making you want to give up and take a drink, just to make the symptoms stop. This is a huge red flag that most probably indicates addiction.

I have an uncle who can drink and never show any effects from it. He seems the same whether or not he is drinking; I do not think I have ever seen him drunk. My uncle is a hit-and-miss drinker; he doesn't drink every day, not even every weekend. He may drink on a holiday or a special occasion. I would consider him a social drinker who, if he decided to stop drinking for a month, would have few to no problems. His body chemistry is such that alcohol does not bother him much.

Now my mother, his sister, on the other hand, will become quite tipsy on just one drink. She also only drinks on occasion, simply because she knows her tolerance is terrible. She is a social drinker, but restricts her drinking to sipping a single drink at an event. My grandfather, however, drank every day for years. Although he never became tipsy, when he had to abstain from drinking for medical reasons, it was sheer hell going through detox.

Because each person responds to alcohol differently, it is very difficult for you to figure out for yourself whether you are a social drinker or you are addicted to alcohol. Here are a few scenarios:

Let's say your kids, aged three and five years old, are playing and little Bobby gets cranky, as do most three-year olds when they don't get their own way or need a nap. Bobby starts crying because his brother has a favorite toy and won't give it to him. A fight ensues and you have to break it up and send the kids to their respective rooms. You want a drink to calm your nerves. The kids are quiet in their rooms. You don't usually drink when things get chaotic, it is just this day. You grab the vodka from under the cupboard and pour just a little into a glass and drink it. That is it, you don't drink anything else and you don't do this every time the kids get into a fight. If you fit into this scenario, you probably don't have a problem with alcohol. It would only be a problem if your spouse came home night after night to find you draped over the bed in a drunken stupor.

In this second example, your boss accuses you of not doing your job well and forgetting to submit an important report that was due several days ago. You know you didn't do what you were supposed to do and you blame it on just about anything you can think of, including other co-workers. At lunch, you find yourself at the local bar having a drink to calm your nerves instead of eating a nutritious meal. This is the third time this week that you visited the bar over the lunch hour, just to get a drink to help you cope with being treated unfairly at work. If you identify with this situation, you have a problem with drinking. You are using alcohol as a crutch and blaming everyone but yourself for your inadequacies.

Although the two scenarios should both send up red flags, the mom who only occasionally imbibes to calm her nerves is probably not addicted. She only wants a drink and she may or may not actually take one. The person with problems at work who has been to the bar for the past four lunch hours definitely has problems.

The difference here is between needing and wanting a drink. If you want a drink, but can take it or leave it, you probably do not have an addiction. If you need a drink after lunch every day because of work pressures, you should pay attention to your behavior, because you are probably addicted.

It is important to note that any type of alcohol can be addictive. The guy who drinks 10 beers a night is just as addicted as the lady who guzzles down three to four glasses of wine in an evening or the man who goes to the bar for eight shots of whiskey. It doesn't matter what you drink. You can get just as addicted to alcohol using fancy ice wine as you can to cheap Strawberry Hill.

Detox Symptoms To Watch

As stated before, you may not experience any withdrawal symptoms at all from alcohol. Your symptoms may be extremely light and inconsequential. This would lead me to believe that you truly are a social drinker who does not have an addiction.

My dad knew firsthand about addiction. His father was an alcoholic, so because of that, plus the fact that a few of his brothers were also hooked on alcohol, he avoided it. I think he only had one or two drinks a year at New Years Eve and Christmas Eve. If he decided he wanted to swear off alcohol entirely, he would have suffered very little.

His sister had a few beers every weekend. Once she started gaining weight because of it, she decided to stop. She had very mild symptoms and the detox process did not bother her much. Another brother was a heavy drinker and because of legal issues was forced into recovery. He experienced withdrawal symptoms so severe that he had to be hospitalized. So, you can see, the extent of alcohol's effects on you will depend on how much you drink as well as your metabolism.

Withdrawal

Withdrawal symptoms usually begin to appear about six to eight hours after you have taken your last drink, but they can surface as early as two hours later. Withdrawal symptoms are at their peak between 24 and 48 hours after your last drink and will start to dissipate in five to seven days. The following are symptoms you need to watch for:

•Cravings for a drink can get pretty intense even after a few hours of not having anything. Try to distract yourself from those cravings as best you can and drink soft drinks or water with some citrus added. Ice tea is refreshing, too.

•Tremors in hands and legs – Also called delirium tremens or DTs, these tremors can be mild to serious. Most people do experience DTs from alcohol withdrawal, but it is seldom severe. They can be lethal however, so it is nothing to fool around with. During DTs you may feel confused, irritable, angry, depressed, or anxious and you may experience nightmares. You may have a headache, nausea and vomiting, and you might sweat profusely. This last is one of the first symptoms of withdrawal to appear.

•Falls are frequent when detoxing, mostly because of the destabilizing nature of DTs. That is another reason you'll want someone around to keep an eye on you during this time.

•Dehydration is a common problem during withdrawal, mostly because it is very hard for the stomach to stand even water. However, you must try to stay hydrated. Water is your best option, but it might be hard to swallow. Fizzy water can sometimes relieve the upset stomach, at least a little. If you suspect dehydration is serious and you can't stop vomiting, it is best to go to an emergency room. You have not failed if you need medical help, you just need help. Do not be too proud to get that help if you need it. It is better to get help than to be dead.

•Hallucinations might appear at around 12 to 24 hours into the withdrawal. This is another reason you want someone to be with you during detoxification. The hallucinations can be very mild. You may find yourself standing in front of the refrigerator and can't remember how you got there or why you are there. You might also have some nasty hallucinations and feel your life is in danger. Severe hallucinations are nothing to fool with. They are another valid reason to head for the emergency room.

•Seizures are a possibility from 24 to 48 hours into detoxification. About two to three percent of individuals who go through detox experience some form of seizure, often brought on by dehydration. Seizures may involve convulsions and falling, but they may also consist of just staring into space or being unable to respond to stimulus. If you go into convulsions your friend should call for emergency help. The best thing a helper can do if you are convulsing is to roll you onto your side and stay with you, preventing you from banging into anything that could hurt you.

Go To The Hospital

If you have any of the following symptoms, be safe and get to the hospital:

•Temperature above 101 degrees Fahrenheit

•Pulse rate of 115 or more – download a pulse rate monitor to your smart phone. They work pretty accurately.

•Systolic blood pressure of 170 or higher.

•Severe dehydration – not being able to keep anything down for eight hours or more.

•Convulsive seizures.

•Uncontrollable hallucinations

Do not take the chance of harm from any of the above.

I am not trying to frighten you out of your month of abstinence, but I would be remiss if I did not let you know what is possible during an alcohol detox. I certainly don't want any harm to come to any of my readers.

In most cases, your symptoms will not be severe; mine weren't that bad. I experienced DTs for a while but they were tolerable. I had no hallucinations, seizures, high temperature, or racing heart problems. My craving for a drink was pretty intense, but I had someone there with me who distracted me from it most of the time.

The experience of detoxing is uncomfortable to be sure, but remember that nothing good ever comes cheap. You can do this; you'll be glad later, if not now.

Do your homework so nothing will be a surprise. This includes exploring methods of sobriety. There are many from which to choose and you can try one or do a combination of several. We will explore some of these methods in the chapters that follow. This will give you some help in forming your own action plan for drinking cessation.

It is important you understand what could happen. You may be one of the lucky ones who have no problems at all, but then again, your body could react to the detoxification process in any number of ways. It's extremely important that you watch for the warning signs and get help immediately if necessary. Detox symptoms can escalate quickly, with deadly results. Don't become a statistic. You want to be able to enjoy your friends, your family, and your life for a long time.

Why do we do strange things after drinking alcohol?

This is one of the key factors that helps the people around us know when we are drinking. One of the biggest aspects of alcohol that makes it attractive to people is that it is a relaxant, and that it helps to reduce our inhibitions. However, this same 'positive' aspect of alcohol is also an incredibly big negative. People are not themselves when they drink, and they can often do things or say things that are out of character. Not only is the behavior strange, it can also be damaging and dangerous.

Perhaps this lack of inhibitions is the reason why people continue to drink. The fact that you feel like you could say or do anything without looking foolish is strong enough a reason to drink more and feel even more courageous in a social situation.

After a few drinks, with inhibitions disappearing fast, drinkers will talk more, become rowdy, and generally act very different to normal. They will then experience a feeling of being 'high'. They are not in fact high, but instead their nervous system is slowly being brought to a standstill.

These early stages are the 'bits that people remember' most fondly. You have a couple of drinks, and then you feel braver, more socially capable, and able to be more of an extrovert. The initital effects of drinking alcohol include:

● Relaxation

● An increased sense of well-being

● Lowered alertness

● A loss of inhibition

● A feeling of elation

And all of the above are the result of just a couple of drinks.

Because our nerves are being affected directly by the alcohol, and because it is initially such a pleasant feeling, we keep drinking until we get to the later stages of intoxication, where we start to stagger around a bit, and lose control of our words and so on.

This can lead to quite embarrassing situations where behaviour becomes so uninhibited that we act in ways that our friends would not expect us to.

If we drive through the city streets at night and see people who have drunk a lot, it will not be uncommon to see them crying, running around in a chaotic fashion, starting arguments and being partially dressed. This is all behaviour that results directly from drinking too much.

We act in this way because one of the main effects of alcohol on our body is a lack of inhibition. This has always been the case. Human beings love believing they have no inhibitions, even if it is just for a couple of hours, and then act accordingly.

Can we drink while taking medication?

There are plenty of people out there who swear that drinking while taking medication is highly dangerous. And it is, if you drink a lot while taking medication.

The reality is that doctors do tell us not to drink while we are on medication. They never really tell us why, but they certainly tell us.

Why do they do this? They do it because they don't want alcohol to interfere with effectiveness of the medication. It is certainly the case that with some drugs you most definitely shouldn't drink, but with the majority of drugs, it is pretty safe to drink in moderation.

Because alcohol is a depressant, it affects the way your brain works. And because many medications are depressants or have sedative qualities, they affect the way your brain works too.

This can mean that you have two substances inside your body, reducing your brain's ability to respond to warning signals about danger, or to even create useful thoughts.

It can also mean that alcohol can directly reduce the impact of the drugs that you are taking. It can lessen the impact, and therefore affect the recovery time that would have been expected. Alcohol can also have such a negative impact upon the drug that it affects your health.

This all becomes a lot more dangerous when you take medication that is meant to help you sleep or relax. The impact of both alcohol and the sedative that you have ingested will make you drowsier quicker and possibly put you in grave danger.

With antibiotics, the picture is a little different. Some antibiotics, when used with alcohol, can cause a number of side effects to be present. Many antibiotics with an alcohol input can give you nausea and flushing, for example.

Some can even lead to accelerated heart rate, alongside shortness of breath. If you already have a heart condition or if you are asthmatic, these conditions can be worsened considerably and perhaps even lead to death.

When it comes to drinking and medication, always consult your doctor first. They do know best. And if they say don't drink, don't drink.

What does 'at risk' drinking mean?

At risk drinking is simply a type of drinking behavior where you and/or the people around you are concerned about the amount of drinking you do, or the nature of the drinking you do.

For men the situation is different than it is for women. Women traditionally have problems drinking as much as men, who have a larger capacity for alcohol than women do. This means that any recognised and respected drinking guide (or a guide as to how many drinks a person can have) will reflect the difference between genders. This section will look at the different limits that both genders have when it comes to alcohol.

For men any more than five drinks a night during a drinking session is considered to be at risk drinking. If you drink more than fourteen drinks a week you are again considered to be a high risk drinker. This means that the majority of drinkers are not necessarily considered to be 'high-risk', because the majority of adults simply do not drink that much.

Women have a lower tolerance and a corresponding lower limit for drinking. Women are expected to have no more than four drinks a night, with the weekly limit coming in at seven drinks a week.

However, it is important that people know what these drinkers are 'at risk' of. Exceeding these limits leaves you vulnerable to developing alcohol dependency or alcohol abuse traits. This is of course a difficult situation to be in, because if not managed carefully, this can lead to alcoholism.

Anyone who binge drinks regularly, as in drinking quickly and intensely during a session, is at high risk of developing an alcohol disorder. If you feel that you are in a situation where you are drinking too much, or that your drinking is becoming something that is out of control, than you should seek the help of a medical professional.

At risj drinking is something that you really need to address, and what follows is an outline of classic management of st risk drinking.

Some steps to take

Set a drinkning goal and make sure that you stic to it. Thsi means looking at your drinking and then setting clear goals that will help you gain some control over the drinking.

If you say that you will only drink two days a week, stick to it and tehn reward yourself when you meet that goal. This way you will experience success, and also move towards reducing your at-risk behaviour.

One excellent way to gain an understanding of just how dangerous your drinking is becoming is to keep a diary. This way, you can log the amount of drinking you do. It is important to be honest with your diary. Literally record the number of drinks you have in the diary on a daily basis, and then look at it after around three weeks. Three weeks is a pattern, and your drinking will fit into a pattern that is best 'readable' after this period of time.

You may be surprised at just how much drinking you end up doing in just three weeks. People are often shocked at the amount of alcohol they introduce into their system over a period of time.

Once your diary has run its' three week course, compare the diary to the goals you have set yourself. Would your goal (if it was met) put you in a better position healthwise?

All the while, make sure that your home becomes a place where alcohol is never present. This means every part of your home is free from drink. Even if you have a drinks cabinet at home that you use for social gatherings, you need to make sure that it is empty of the alcohol. This is absolutelty vital if you want to cut down on that at risk drinking.

You can also do a lot more when it comes to your behaviour when you are drinking. If you are an at risk drinker, you are basically drinking in a dangerous fashion. So the obvious behaviour that you need to put in place is that which promotes drinking in a safe and responsible fashion.

Sip your drinks carefully and slowly. Don't race through your drinks so the effect hits you quicker. That is not the point when it comes to responsible drinking.

You can also ensure that you take a break between drinks of one hour. This allows your body to deal with the effect of alcohol in a manageable way. This is a sensible way of managing the inflow of alcohol to the body.

Finally, a good piece of advice for any at risk drinker is to pick one day of the week when you make sure that you do not drink at all. It is absolutely important that you do this before you do anything else, especially if you are finding it difficult to stop drinking overall. Then stop for a week and note your feelings. The more you do this the more you will be able to 'see the forest for the trees'.

# Chapter 10: Ego

In hindsight is where you'll often discover the hidden wisdom in things you've heard or read. Especially biblical passages; where you've heard and read them so many times, you only understand them for what they seem to be on the surface. Nowhere is this irony more pertinent than in this chapter. I remind you that the principles in this book are not based in religion, but the message in Matthew 7:5 is perfect for our purposes here.

"You hypocrite! First take the beam out of your own eye, and then you will see clearly to remove the speck from your brother's eye."

You've heard this one, haven't you? What does it mean? Basically, it's a reminder to clean up your own mess before you start criticizing others for theirs—generally good advice. But let's look at why it needed to be said. Why is it that we tend to be so hypocritical?

It's not that we're bad people for wanting to help others before we help ourselves. There's nothing bad about that at all. And there's a good reason why we do it, hypocritical as it may be.

Picture this: a close friend of yours is in bad shape. She's overweight, has high blood sugar, high cholesterol, high blood pressure; the whole enchilada. She has a sedentary lifestyle, eats fast food; generally makes the wrong decisions. She'd love to lose weight and get in shape; she's told you numerous times, yet she's never seemed to do anything about it. You've always treaded lightly around the subject of her making changes, but at this point, you realize you've been doing her no favors by being so polite. Besides, you know exactly what she needs to do to improve her health (for the purpose of this example, let's say you're an expert on the subject). So all she needs to do is follow your instructions, and she can change her life forever.

You write her a simple meal plan and a simple exercise plan. Eat these healthy meals, perform these simple workouts a couple times a week, and by this time next year, Sandy, you should be a whole different woman.

Again, for the purpose of this example, let's assume you're right on the money. If she follows your advice, she'll get exactly the results she desires. She'll lose all the weight. Hell, she'll turn into a supermodel. She'll marry a rich man. She'll add years to her life. I'm talking a complete turnaround. Your advice is no less than solid gold.

So, what do you suppose is going to happen? Even though your advice is certainly worth following, is that any guarantee that she'll follow it?

Not at all. If she's like most people, maybe she'll follow it for a week or two, then she'll slip up. Soon she'll come up with a reason why she just can't do it. She'll say she isn't ready, or this particular plan is just not for her. She'll say she doesn't have time to work out. She can't afford the healthy food. The salad took too long to chew.

Why? When your way was unquestionably and exponentially better, the question is why?

The answer to this question is one that deserves careful examination. Writing it off as a lack of will power is a big mistake, and an excuse you'll use for yourself when you refuse to follow good advice. There's an incredibly important, yet incredibly elusive reason why people sabotage themselves like this, and it's one you'll need to fully understand to disable the power it exercises over you. When you do, you'll understand why this whole business of "beams in people's eyes" is such an issue, even with everyone so hypocritically trying to help each other. There's nothing wrong with the advice you gave to Sandy; even if you are struggling with exactly the same problems as she is, it's still great advice worth following.

We all have our demons. I assume, since you picked up this book, that yours is alcohol. Don't feel bad—it's mine too. I assume that you, as I have, have come to realize that your drinking is a problem. You're right. Whether you've gotten to the point where you need it to be happy, or can't seem to go to bed without it, or your liver values are elevated, or you're tired of the aching in your dehydrated kidneys, or you already know the pleasure of having liters of yellow fluid drained by a siphon screwed into your viscera, you're correct. You've reached a fork in the road. Not to be dramatic, but here's the truth: down the road you're currently on awaits depression, disappointment, and death. It doesn't get any better, only worse. As long as you're still moving in the wrong direction, you can count on becoming one of the 2.5 million people a year who die early, undignified deaths from alcohol-related illnesses. If you've ever been lucky enough to witness one of these taking place, you already know how sad and gruesome it is.

For me, it was my father. He died at 61. But with his bloated, yellow corpse-like body sprawled on the living room sofa for as long as it was, when the time came, it felt to me that he'd already been dead for months. He was helpless, practically comatose, unable to speak the words he wanted to say. I mean, he was really gone. Really pitiful. Death came soon after; by then, to everyone's relief.

Now, this was a man who sped-read several dictionary-sized non-fiction books a week. He had two Master's degrees and a Doctorate degree in French Baroque Opera. No, I'm not kidding. He was a freak genius. I'm willing to assume, in fact, that he was a hell of a lot smarter than our hypothetical friend, Sandy. He was also very aware of the consequences of drinking; he didn't need anyone's golden advice. He also had all the chances in the world to stop before it killed him.

Considering all of this, let's return to the big question—why?

There must be a force in play. A powerful one, with an uncanny ability to override proper reasoning in even the most intelligent human beings. It is not an intelligence issue that causes us to behave so irrationally. Nor is it lack of intelligence that causes us to be so hypocritical—to be fully aware what is best for other people, yet still ignore the beams in our own eyes.

This biblical warning, (at least for our purposes) isn't about pontification itself, let alone a mote of irritating sawdust in your friend's eye. It's a warning about a profoundly powerful component of our personalities; hinted at here well-before Sigmund Freud developed his structural model of the human psyche. It's called the Ego.

Established Facts:

We may be hypocritical with our sage advice to others, but it just goes to show that we know what is best for ourselves as well.

You are not stupid for being an addict. The force of the ego is so powerful, even the smartest people have drank themselves to death.

# Chapter 11: Signs Of Alcoholism

Alcohol habits could be challenging to recognize, unlike cocaine or heroin; alcohol is accessible and its consumption accepted in lots of cultures. It's often the core of interpersonal relations, and it's usually connected with celebrations and pleasure.

Drinking is an integral part of some people's lives, for some, it's gotten from the culture, however, it's hard to differentiate between someone who takes alcohol seldomly and those addicted to it.

Some symptoms of alcohol addiction are:

Increase in quantity intake.

High tolerance for alcohol.

Drinking alcohol at inappropriate times and places.

Wanting to be where lots of alcohol are e.g, a gathering, party, etc.

Change in friendship: someone who loves alcohol may also choose friends who drink heavily.

Avoiding interactions with family members.

Hiding and denying that you drink alcohol.

Depending on alcohol to work or engage in activities.

Legal or professional problems such as an arrest or losing a job.

As addiction gets worse after a while, you must recognize early enough the signs of addiction (if recognized and treated early), someone addicted to liquor would probably deny it's symptoms.

If you're worried that someone you know is addicted to alcohol, avoid shaming them or making them feel guilty; this might drive them away or even make them resist your support but rather encourage and reassure them.

Medical Conditions Associated with Alcoholism

Alcohol addiction can result in coronary and liver disease, it might also cause:

Ulcer.

Diabetes.

Sexual problems.

Congenital disabilities.

Bone loss.

Eye problem.

Increased risk of cancer.

Suppressed immune function.

Someone with alcohol addiction can unknowingly put others in danger because of their unconscious state. Based on statistics from the Centres for Disease Control and Avoidance (CDC), about 28000 people in the U.S have died as a result of suicide and homicide, which is relatively due to alcoholism.

These problems adequately explains why it is necessary to deal with alcohol addiction early. Virtually all problems associated with alcohol yearnings could be avoidable or treated with long-term recovery.

Treatment Plans for Alcoholism?

Treating alcohol addiction could be complicated and challenging. For the treatment to work, the person with an addiction should abstain from alcohol as much as they can or reduce its intake; you can't pressure them into not drinking if they aren't ready. Successful treatment is solely dependent on the person's desire to become better.

The healing process of alcoholism can be a long-term commitment; there is absolutely no immediate solution, and it involves daily care; as a result of this, many people say those with alcoholism never get "healed."

Rehab

A typical treatment option for someone with alcohol addiction is an outpatient or inpatient treatment. An inpatient program can last from thirty days to one year; it usually reduces drawback symptoms and psychological difficulties. Outpatient treatment provides daily support and allows the patient to come from home.

Alcoholics Anonymous and other Organizations

Individuals who depend on alcohol and need to help themselves might consider the 12-step program like Alcoholics Anonymous (AA); some organizations don't follow the 12-step model but opt for Wise Recovery and Sober Recovery.

Whatever the support system, it's good to at least stay sober, the sobriety will help anyone fighting alcohol addiction. A friendly atmosphere might also proffer relatable experiences and offer good and healthy support; these things help an alcohol addict and provide them with a comfortable environment when there's a relapse.

Other Options

Someone with alcohol addiction may also have the advantage of several treatments such as:

Drug therapy.

Counseling.

Nutritional changes.

Doctors may prescribe drugs to help with certain conditions, e.g, antidepressants. Antidepressants work well if the alcohol addict is on self-medication to deal with his/her depression or if the doctors prescribe drugs to assist with other conditions associated with recovery.

It is easy to attend therapy sessions to help one on how best to control any risk of strain in recovery and the need to prevent a relapse. Also, healthy eating can help undo whatever harm alcoholism might have done to a person's health, like regaining lost weight.

Treating alcoholism may involve different treatment plans. An addict should get one of these recovery programs that may support long-term sobriety; this might be a therapy session for a person who is usually depressed.

Where can one find help for Alcoholism?

For more information about alcoholism or to help someone you love seek options for help, it would be advisable to talk to a doctor. They can refer you for local programs, such as centers or the 12-step program. Also, the following organizations could be of help:

National Council on Alcoholism and Medication Dependence (NCADD).

National Institute on Alcohol consumption Abuse and Alcoholism (NIAAA).

National Institute on Drug abuse.

Drug abuse and Mental Health Services Administration.

What's the perspective on alcoholism?

Early treatment of alcohol addiction is advisable because addictions that have gone longer are harder to break; however, effective treatment is designed for long-term habits.

Relatives and families of people who are addicted to alcohol can help them get professional help or register for programs like Al-Anon.

Someone with alcohol addiction who has remained sober for weeks or years may suddenly realize they are having a relapse; and this could be a result of binge drinking. Eventually, sobriety may be the obligation of anyone addicted to alcohol; it's essential to never encourage harmful behaviors and to maintain appropriate limitations if the addict continues to drink; this might mean cutting off financial assistance if it will make it difficult for them to satisfy their craving.

If someone you love is an addict; endeavor to be motivating and provide emotional support.

# Chapter 12: Impact Of Alcoholism

## On Humanity

The impact of alcoholism on the family could be financial, emotional, physical, and even religious. Alcoholism affects the entire family, not only by being distressing but also by creating loss and trauma. Several American families that have been torn apart by this fatal disease will attest to this, the impact of alcoholism on the family is universally negative.

The physiological symptoms of alcohol abuse include flushed skin, slurred speech, and imbalanced steps; other dangers of alcohol abuse are injuries, DUI, and reckless behavior. Those fighting alcoholism succumb to drinking only in private, hangovers, blackouts, mood swings, or irritability that often accompanies drinking. The family may also discover additional troubling traits.

A common side-effect of alcohol abuse is aggression and violent behavior. Subsequently, those who drink regularly are likely to be hostile and may not be united with their family. If someone drunk from alcohol drives, they can injure themselves or others and sustain severe injuries, putting another life in danger. Death can happen which can tear the family apart.

Juvenile Drinking and Family Friction

Adolescent drinking is another problem that affects many American adults. They might be in a variety of degrees of development and sometimes have a problem managing public and emotional stress. Peer pressure often stimulates drinking, as friends offer alcohol without judgment. Early juvenile consumption can create a first alcohol tolerance; thereby, encouraging more alcohol consumption.

By the time the student enters high school, they could have an increased tolerance or a high reliance on alcohol. Parents may find it difficult to connect with their children because they now talk to kids who have started drinking and experimenting with drugs. Most of all, they may rebel when there's a law they can't conform to in the family thereby causing friction among family members.

Alcoholism and Financial Strains on the Family

The impact of addiction on households can last for a long time regardless of the difference between different types of alcoholism; alcohol consumption can impact family and friends. Alcohol's ability to change one's brain and go directly into one's bloodstream makes it a robust but destructive habit to indulge. Individuals who drink will overspend as drinking can cost quite a lot of money. Due to the damage of alcohol, as well as the rate of relapse, someone can spend between $20 or $300 per round.

Once someone is intoxicated, they can lose complete control over their money. As a result of this, the money they spend on drinks instead of paying bills can be extremely straining to the family.

Adults who have problems with alcohol consumption dependency can avoid duties such as work and family responsibilities. Likewise, they can have poor job performance, risking job loss, allowing their family to suffer financial reductions because they are accountable to them.

How Alcohol affects Pregnant Women

Prenatal alcohol abuse is a normal occurrence that harms the mother as well as the developing fetus. Any amount of alcohol during pregnancy is risky. As a result of this, babies whose mothers have been drinking are taken care of specially at delivery. This is because they might be born with certain qualities which are due to their mothers' alcohol intake, these qualities are referred to as Fatal Alcohol consumption Symptoms, such as:

Small heads.

Shorter stature.

Lower torso weight.

Disability.

Behavioral problems.

Heart problems

One out of ten pregnant women who drink, increase their rate of alcoholism after childbirth. Furthermore, they might endanger healthy family through their psychological and behavioral symptoms of alcohol abuse such as:

Aggression.

Stress reaction.

Isolation.

Low self-esteem.

Financial loss.

Mood swings.

Irritability

Get Help Today

Alcoholism can be a hereditary habit that affects the entire family in different ways. Treatment experts can help those fighting addictions by providing the best service specialized in re-establishing broken relationships while healing takes place.

The Five Types of Alcoholics

There is a stereotype in the use of alcohol. However, a written report from the Countrywide Institute on Alcoholic beverages Misuse and Alcoholism (NIAAA), Countrywide Institute of Health (NIH), as well as the Countrywide Epidemiological Report on Alcohol consumption and Related Conditions (NESARC) put that idea to rest. These organizations conducted a nationwide clinical study based on assorted studies on alcoholics. The analysis revealed that you will find five subtypes of alcoholics:

Young Adult Subtype.

Functional Subtype.

Intermediate Familial Subtype.

Young Antisocial Subtype.

Chronic Severe Subtype

These subtypes are categories predicated on the age of the average person, when they started drinking when they developed alcohol dependence, their history of alcoholism, the existence of reoccurring mental medical issues, as well as the presence of other alcohol abuse disorders. They aren't designed like a diagnosis to find out whether someone is experiencing alcoholism, instead, they are designed to improve analysis on addiction and guide future research and avoidance efforts.

Alcoholics are affected for different reasons; some people may not even realize that their drinking is a problem; rather, they see it as an integral part of their lives. However, regardless of your age, position, or family, alcoholism can create long-term conditions that may damage your overall health and relationships, regardless of your subtype.

Young Adult Subtype

Whatever the stereotype, almost all those who fall in these five types of alcoholics are young. It is placed that roughly 31.5% of alcoholics are adults, which may be the largest single group. This group starts drinking early(about age 19) and also, develops alcohol consumption dependency early (about 24). This group has comparatively low rates of re-occurring mental medical issues and moderate rates of other substance abuse disorders and families with alcoholism.

The young adult subtype is less likely to have a full-time job and is more likely to have more college students than other groups and they are less likely to be married.

This subtype consumes alcohol less than other groups but is usually prone to binge drinking when they are drinking. Members of the group are 2.5 times more likely to be males than females. Though it is unlikely that someone in this group will seek treatment, they will probably look for a 12-Step program if they need one.

Functional Subtype

The Functional subtype is the same as "functional alcoholics." Having about 19.5% of alcoholics, this is the group that's keeping down jobs and relationships; this group is often middle-aged (around 41). Members of the group start drinking early (about 18) and develop alcohol consumption dependency (around age 37). This group experiences mild depression, but lower rates of other reoccurring disorders; many members of the group smoke cigars, but few have other substance use disorders, and about 60% of the group are men.

Of all subtypes, the functional subtype is minimal, and are likely to have legal problems, and are also less likely to have drinking issues. They have the very best education levels and income than other groups of alcoholics and half of this group are married. They may be individuals who can have control over what goes on in their lives. However, while they are "practical" in ways, they constantly crave for alcohol. Less than 20% of this subgroup needs help, and most of them get it from the 12-Step program or a private doctor.

Intermediate Familial Subtype

The familial subtype has about 18.8% of alcoholics. This group appears to start drink as teens (around 17) and also become an alcoholic dependent around age 32; this subgroup is likely to have a family member with alcoholism. They have a high possibility of experiencing anti-social personality disorder, depression, panic, and bipolar disorder. This group experiences high rates of cigarettes, cannabis, and cocaine obsession.

The familial subtype is 64% male; this group has an increased education level than most, however, not up to the functional subtype. Members of the group have full-time careers than other groups, but their income level is lower than the practical subtype. While this group isn't likely to get treatment, those that do have a tendency to head to self-help groups, niche treatment programs, cleansing programs, and private healthcare providers.

Young Antisocial Subtype

This group starts drinking very early, around age fifteen and about 21.1% of alcoholics fall into this subtype. They grow into alcohol consumption dependency at age eighteen. More than 50% of these groups have traits of anti-social personality disorder. There are also high rates of depression, bipolar disorder, interpersonal phobia, and obsessive-compulsive disorder. This group offers the best prices for other substance abuse, including reliance on cigarettes, weed, meth, cocaine, and opioids, and more than 3/4 of its members are male.

This group has the lowest form of education, employment, and income than any group; they also indulge in alcohol more than other groups, although they drink somewhat less frequently than usual. Alternatively, this group is likely to need help than other alcoholic groups, with 35% having sought help in overcoming alcoholism. This group gets the best treatment from a special doctor, but also often chooses self-help groupings, specialization treatment programs, and detoxification programs.

Chronic Severe Subtype

The chronic severe subtype makes up about the smallest percentage of alcoholics, with just 9.2%. This group is inclined to start drinking at age 15 but typically becomes alcoholic dependent at 29. 77% of the group have close families with alcoholism while 47% of it's members show anti-social personality disorder, which is higher than any subtype. This subtype may be prone to depression, dysthymia, bipolar disorder, panic, sociable phobia, and panic disorders. This group is likely to be dependent on cannabis, cocaine, and opioids.

More than 80% of the group encounters severe alcohol withdrawal and a consistent attempt to quit, and more than 90% drink whenever they are confronted with a problem, they engage in binge drinking and spend several hours drinking. Most of their time is devoted to drinks and most of them develop alcohol disorder dependency.

This group has the highest number of divorce and separation cases, they have the lowest level of education, and also earn the lowest income, this group drinks more regularly than almost every other group, although their total alcohol intake is less than the young antisocial subtype. 66% of this group might seek support with regards to alcoholism, making them the most liable to seek help.

They often seek advice at self-help organizations, treatment programs, and cleansing programs. They get the best treatment at an inpatient program and also consult private doctors, psychiatrists, and cultural employees for help at high prices.

What's the End Stage of Alcoholism?

People fighting End-Stage Alcoholism frequently have many Complications. End-stage alcoholism is the ultimate stage of addiction, and maybe the most damaging. A person reaches end-stage alcoholism after a long time of alcohol abuse. At this point, people who have spent years drinking may have issues with numerous medical health insurance and mental conditions, due to their abuse of alcohol. The average individuals may isolate themselves, lose their job, or damage important organs in their bodies.

What are the Stages of Alcoholism?

Alcohol abuse has many phases; the degrees of alcohol misuse are split into six categories. These are:

Social Drinking

The first stage is social drinking; i.e a comparatively non-threatening degree of drinking, which can not necessarily result in alcohol misuse. It's drinking when out with friends.

Binge Drinking

Another stage is binge drinking, this is a common practice influencing one out of every six American adults, Americans drink 17 billion alcohol each year. Binge drinking could be short-term, or happen frequently, signaling the chance of potential massive drinking or alcohol abuse.

Heavy Drinking

Another stage is heavy consumption. At this stage, the individual has more craving for alcohol. They drink frequently, every day, or drink extreme amounts when drinking socially. Taking more than five drinks in 2 hours is common in this stage.

Alcohol Dependency

The fourth stage is alcohol dependency. At this stage, the drinker is dependent on alcohol to live "normally" and may experience negative symptoms or emotions when they aren't drinking. This dependency may be rooted in psychological and mental motivations.

**Addiction/Alcoholism**

The fifth stage has a total dependence on alcohol. The person is now an alcoholic, they start to exhibit several behaviors that affect their health, personal and professional lives. For example, alcoholics will continue to drink regardless of how much it affects them negatively.

End-Stage Alcoholism

Lastly, this stage is referred to as the end-stage of alcohol abuse, it is the stage where the alcoholic is experiencing severe health and mental issues and could encounter the risk of death.

End-Stage Alcoholism and Health Complications

End-Stage Alcoholism is quite serious; it usually poses a lot of health challenges. Initial, the liver becomes damaged, partially or completely. The liver gains fat and starts to swell, eventually leading to liver scarring. The damage to the liver is called liver disease or cirrhosis.

The damaged liver could cause other problems in the body since it is an essential organ. The liver is in charge of several tasks within the body, it is to ensure that the body works as healthy as possible. Other health issues like cardiovascular disease and heart stroke stem from chronic alcohol abuse in end phases of alcoholism. Risks of dementia and malignancy also increase; even brain damage and hepatitis can happen in the end-stage of alcoholism.

# Chapter 13: Diet For Recovery

A good idea will also be to plan a new diet. Often people with alcohol problems will not have had a good diet. Alcohol was the most important thing. It was more important to feel intoxicated than to feel like with a full stomach. Many of us put premium fuel on our cars but don't think much about what we put in our bodies. What we put in it plays a big role in how we feel during the day on how we think. Start treating you body better and respect it. Alcohol is a toxin and so is bad food. You will feel tremendous change by switching to a healthier diet. Nobody is saying you have to go Cold-Turkey on this. You can slowly start switching out for example snackbars with fruits.

Start slowly. This is not a 3 week diet. You decided to quit drinking for life right? This is also for life. If you only want to do this short-term you are only fooling yourself. Do it the right way. If you start slowly by switching out the bad with something more healthy you have better chance of succeeding and making this long-term. You will also look better! Who doesn't want that? Fruits and vegetables should be around 30% of your diet. Try to go more into organic food as it hasn't been sprayed with pesticides and other toxins. The better you feel the less of an urge you will have for alcohol.

As alcohol has alot of calories (only fat has more) people that have been drinking for a while don't have a big sense of hunger even though that have not eaten much. This is because alcohol affects sensors in the brain that cause the hunger feeling. Because of this bad diet drinkers may have experienced poor appetite, poor food digestion, constipation and diarrhea. In this case they need a more healthy diet and specially food that has a lot of nutrients to build up tissues that may have been damaged and organs that my operate poorly of years of drinking and abuse.

Studies show that a good diet and healthy nutrition can be a big help when it comes to the recovery of addicts that are struggling with the craving of alcohol. It also affects the mood the diet you are on. Coffee intake and a lot of sugar should be avoided or minimised in the beginning as it can cause mood swings. Sugar is to be avoided because it can cause cravings in the long-term, anxiety, diabets and imbalance in the hormones.

A good balance in the diet would be around 30 percent fat, 45 percent carbohydrate and 26 percent protein. It's a good idea to eat more complex carbohydrates that are longer to digest and that provide a longer and stable energy with fewer urges to turn to drinking.

Protein is a good nutrition for rebuilding tissues and key to fixing the liver and other organs that may have been affected through the years of drinking. Red meat, chicken, fish and eggs should be high on your diet list when it comes to protein intake. If you need a quick snack than nuts are a good protein source.

Articial foods should be avoided as it causes stress on the liver which is has enough workload just by breaking down preservatives and chemicals. Try to eat as natural as possible. Go Gluten Free and Paleo. Some people have had good success by cutting out dairy and wheat.

Persistence

Like I said before this journey will not be easy. Nothing that is really worth something is. But that doesn't mean that it can't be done. You will make some mistakes and be tempted. You could even fall into drinking again. DON'T let that ruin you. Even if you fall get into the saddle again. Persistence is king. There are very few things that can beat persistence. People have achieved incredible things in life just by persistence. They have become millionares, olympic winners and great leaders just by not giving up. Very few great people became that way without making mistakes. Everybody makes them. Even though you will make one it's not the end. Stand up and continue. Few mistakes are so big that they can't be corrected. You might even learn something from them. When you decide to look at mistakes of a way to learn and to make yourself better you will not be afraid of doing them anymore. Just try to not do the same one over and over. If you learn from them it's ok. If you show persistence you will come out a winner in the end. So don't give up.

To have persistence you need to have goals. You have probably heard it many times before but it has a lot of truth in it.

Write down your goals. It is a way to manifest them for yourself. It changes things to see concept and ideas on paper because they become solid and "alive". So knowing your goals and writing them down on paper is something you must do to be able to have persistence to reach them.

Next step is to make a time-frame. When do you want to reach these goals? Also you can divide your goal/s into smaller one because it's easier to manage and accomplish small things than bigger ones. By completing small goals you will feel better with yourself and feel like you have made progress which is important when you are beginning.

If you are trying to break bad habits try to set a goal by quitting one a day or one a week. Then just take it step by step. Be aware of the motivation around you. If you see results you should enjoy the attention it gets. Demonstrate it if you would. Have in mind that when you reach some of your goals you can show off your work to others. We all love when other people admire us or envy us and use this for your motivation. Know that when you finish something you can use your results for motivation.

Enjoy the benefits

There are many benefits from quitting drinking and you should enjoy them. First of all and the most obvious one is that you will start saving money very quickly. All that money you used to spend on alcohol is now filling you wallet and you can use that money to do something fun, save it to a fund or pay down debt.

Healing of the brain will start when you quit drinking. If you have been drinking heavily for many years you will probably have been feeling out of energy, not thinking clearly and having trouble focusing. This is what alcohol does to the brain. But if you quit drinking you will start to feel more focused and be able to think more clearly and the fog begins to clear in your brain.

You will no longer have to live in shame. Many people try to hide their drinking because they are ashamed of it so they stash their liquor in closets, shelfes or in various places to hide it from family or friends. You will no longer have to live with this guilt of playing this hiding game. People will have more respect for you and if you have a spouse she will for sure look at you in a new perspective.

You body will also start to feel different and pains you have had in the past will start to go away. Alcohol has the tendendies to magnify pains. I also prevents vitamin absorption. Your face and complexion will improve because drinking can heavily affect the moisture in our skin. When you take out drinking these problems will go away. Also and not least your liver will start to heal and many people say that their vision and mood improves drastically.

Relationships improve. You save money. You dont feel as depressed. You improve at work.

Reward Yourself

This is not an easy journey like I said before so if you are making progress you should reward yourself for your results. You are changing your life in a big way but that doesn't mean that it has to be boring or hard. It's very important for you to treat yourself good because you deserve it. You will make mistakes but it's important for you to forgive yourself for making them and just continue down the road. The key is persistence. No matter how often you fall you should get up again.

You can set small goals for you to accomplish like not drinking for a week or a month. Not going to the bar for one week, going to the gym twice a week. Something small. You can then escalate it further when you have picked up speed. It doesn't have to be anything big. You want to have small victories that eventually lead you to win the war.

If things are going good you could use the money you have saved by not buying alcohol to go maybe and buy new clothes, to go to the cinema or take a short trip somewhere exciting. You could buy a camera and just go out and taking photos. Use your imagination. Do what makes you feel good. Remember. Your life should improve by not drinking. And it will. You will start to enjoy things you thought were unimportant in the past.

# Conclusion

Most people love their families and spouses regardless of hardship and suffering they may experience. People are connected to their loved ones. If your loved one is lying, stealing and hurting themselves or you because of drug or alcohol abuse, do the rules change?

Drug and alcohol abusers forget quickly. Promises and agreements are forgotten.

What are the right ways to rescue a drug addict or alcoholic? Most families believe they are doing the right thing, but are surprised or shocked when a drug or alcohol abusing loved one doesn't respond the way they wanted to.

I hear the same big mistakes being committed by families while trying to save their drug / alcohol abusing loved one. How does one provide a space for addicts to recover without helping them to continue their abusing lifestyle?

If you have a loved one abusing drugs and alcohol and don't know why they continue to abuse despite promising they'll stop, you may be making one or more of these major mistakes.